THE LEXICON OF ADLERIAN PSYCHOLOGY

THE LEXICON OF ADLERIAN PSYCHOLOGY

106 TERMS ASSOCIATED WITH THE INDIVIDUAL PSYCHOLOGY OF ALFRED ADLER

Second edition, revised and expanded

Jane Griffith
Robert L. Powers

Adlerian Psychology Associates Publishers
Floyd, Virginia USA

Library of Congress Copyright Registration Number: TX 6-860-634

ISBN (paper): 978-0-918287-10-6
E-book © 2011: 978-0-918287-11-3

Second edition, revised and expanded

First edition, titled *An Adlerian Lexicon: Fifty-nine Terms Associated with the Individual Psychology of Alfred Adler,* © 1984 by The Americas Institute of Adlerian Studies, Ltd.; 2nd printing, 1987.

Books by the same authors
> *The Individual Psychology Client Workbook with Supplements*
> *The Key to Psychotherapy: Understanding the Self-Created Individual* ©2012 (original work titled *"Understanding Lifestyle"*)

Unless otherwise noted in the text, quotations cited are from *The Individual Psychology of Alfred Adler: A Systematic Presentation in Selections from his Writings,* edited and annotated by Heinz L. Ansbacher and Rowena R. Ansbacher. © 1956, Basic Books, Inc., Publishers. [Paperback, 1964, Harper & Row, Publishers, Inc.] Used by permission of The Perseus Books Group.

Orders: www.adlerianpsychologyassociates.com
Inquiries: jsgrlp@gmail.com

Adlerian Psychology Associates
P.O. Box 605
Floyd, Virginia 24091-0605

DEDICATION

We dedicate this work to the memory of Rowena and Heinz Ansbacher,
for their exemplary scholarship and boundless kindness,
for their leadership and encouragement of two who would emulate them if we could.

Foreword

There are two requirements for writing a lexicon, a complete in-depth knowledge of a subject and linguistic precision. Jane Griffith and Robert L. Powers have a long history in Adlerian Psychology as authors, teachers, and therapists. Their use of language is meticulous.

If you decide to write a lexicon, you need a powerful reason to take on this extraordinarily difficult and demanding chore. In his Introduction to *The Lexicon of Adlerian Psychology* Powers explains their aim: to "contribute to the growing interest in [Adlerian Psychology] by clarifying its distinctive terminology," and "making the value of the Adlerian system of penetrating thought and effective practice more widely understood." They wanted to do a good deed. This *Lexicon* is a good deed, a very good deed.

There are more than 100 entries in this *Lexicon*. My guess is that ninety or so would have been included by any Adlerian scholar asked to develop a list of terms essential to such a text; in other words, those entries one would expect to find are here, enriched by the inclusion of other terms as important, though less frequently encountered. The entries cover the essentials of Individual Psychology theory and therapeutic practice, and provide support for a vast array of applications of Adlerian theory without dwelling on techniques of those practices. I think that anyone who considers him- or herself an Adlerian could benefit from reading *The Lexicon*.

The entries define Adlerian terms. Clarity and precision are the hallmarks of definition. One comes to understand Adlerian terms within one's understanding of the theory. And one finds, at least this one found, that one's understanding and use of some terms had become sloppy. I felt like a veteran soldier, content in his role, called to attention. I had been upright, but now I was straight and focused. When I first learned the theory and the terms I was at attention, but over the years I had become at ease. Reading *The Lexicon*, being reminded of the exact meanings, history, and relations of the terms brought me a renewed clarity, an exactitude, which familiarity had softened. Funnily enough, I think working through *The Lexicon* will be as useful and rewarding for the knowledgeable Adlerian as for the novice.

In that regard, I am not sure but that *The Lexicon* could serve as a text for learning Adlerian Psychology. A difficulty in teaching Adlerian theory is that the theory is a whole, all of its parts are related, and the whole is greater than the sum of the parts. So where do you start? *The Lexicon* places the entries in alphabetical order which does not appear a way to learn about the topic. However, related terms are pointed out for each entry as appropriate, and one could follow these relations around and through *The Lexicon* and cover the theory. Or, a newcomer to Adlerian Psychology could just sit down and read *The Lexicon* and learn the theory by the sheer weight of the meanings of the terms and their relations to each other. I intend to use *The Lexicon* the next time I teach Adlerian theory to see if this is correct.

I am content with and impressed by the definitions and explanations of the terms Griffith and Powers include in *The Lexicon* and I think most North American Adlerians will be also. However, as I have found through attendance and participation at the Congress of the International Association of Individual Psychology every three years for the last fifteen years, that there are quite large and important differences in the understanding and practice of Adlerian Psychology around the world, within and across countries. If this *Lexicon* were presented as the world standard for Adlerian terms and meanings, it would prompt a vigorous discussion which could clarify the differences and necessitate new agreement. This might demand translations of *The Lexicon,* which would be no easy feat, particularly since some of the problems with terms emanates from their translation from German to English. Nonetheless, a common, agreed upon set of Adlerian terms with meanings would go a long way to unifying and strengthening Adlerian theory and practice internationally.

From its most obvious function as a dictionary, to a text, an aide-mémoire, or an international standard or code, Griffith and Powers's *Lexicon* is a useful and welcome contribution.

Guy J. Manaster, Ph.D.
University of Texas at Austin

President, International Association
of Individual Psychology

April 11, 2007

Preface

In this second revised edition of *An Adlerian Lexicon* (with its new name, *The Lexicon of Adlerian Psychology*), readers of the first edition will see that we have expanded and enriched the text by adding a significant number of new terms and by updating original entries.

Entries have been arranged alphabetically in the new edition for greater ease of access (the original text was arranged developmentally).

Quotations not otherwise attributed to their various authors are from A. Adler (1964a), *The Individual Psychology of Alfred Adler,* edited and annotated by Heinz L. and Rowena R. Ansbacher (used with permission of the publisher). Because the preponderance of quotations used here are from this 1964 text, we have cited these quotations with *page numbers only,* as shown here, from the entry titled **MOVEMENT**: All is **movement** (p. 195).

Cross-references to other entries in the text are indicated by means of SMALL CAPITAL LETTERS.

Bold type is used to highlight the topic of each entry when the topic is referred to in the related discussion and quotations.

We have also made numerous corrections in this new edition. Indeed, to our chagrin, we had to start our corrections on *page i* (the preface), where we found we had mislearned and therefore misquoted Adler as having said, "The meaning of life is contribution." We herewith correct this quotation, which should read, "Life means — to contribute to the whole" (p. 153).

Dear Reader, we said then and say again, "We hope by means of this lexicon we are able to make a contribution to your understanding of Individual Psychology."

Jane Griffith
Robert L. Powers

May, 2007
Port Townsend, Washington

CONTENTS

CONTENTS

CONTENTS

CONTENTS

Introduction

What's a lexicon?

— A graduate dean

Her question was sincere, without irony or guile. The dean held a responsible position in an internationally known graduate school. We note her question here because, if the word was strange to her, it is likely to be strange to many people. With her honest question as a caution, it seemed to us fitting to begin our text on words by defining the word with which we named the text.

So, here's the answer: A lexicon is a dictionary. Why then not call this book a dictionary? We could have done that. A wordbook is a wordbook by either name. Then again, there are shades of difference, and a difference in names can imply a difference in character. Things usually expected from a dictionary (as the *diction* part of the name implies) include definitions and other matters of usage, plus a guide to pronunciation, in a list of words arranged alphabetically.

The word *lexicon* has a different nuance in its meaning, one that better serves our purpose and our hope in putting this book forward. We chose the word (to quote *The American Heritage Dictionary of the English Language*) as a "stock of terms used in a particular profession, subject, or style; a vocabulary." *American Heritage* goes on to give, as an example of the way in which the word may be used, "*the lexicon of surrealist art*."

In this case our purpose is to introduce and clarify the meaning of a family of words used by or particular to the Adlerian school of psychological art and understanding; our hope is that we may contribute to the growing interest in this school by clarifying its distinctive terminology, with the further hope of making the value of the Adlerian system of penetrating thought and effective practice more widely understood. If we can do that, we will have made this system less vulnerable to the misrepresentation and consequent disregard it has too often had to endure.

In its first edition, privately published as a help to students, we referred to our work as *An Adlerian Lexicon*. Now, thanks to the enthusiastic reception that initial effort has enjoyed, the many photocopied replicas in active use, and the material we have since accumulated, the day has come in which this present volume can be called *The Lexicon of Adlerian Psychology*. It remains "a stock of terms" used regularly in the writings of Alfred Adler (1870-1937), and of those who have studied and continue to develop his theory and practice.

What's an Adlerian?

— Everyman

This is a question of another order, commonly asked of us and harder to answer. It refers to those who believe they are following in the tradition of the work originated by Alfred Adler, a figure of renown in the history of psychiatry, psychology, and psychotherapy during the first half of the 20th Century. Adler was a general practice physician with a specialty in ophthalmology who, with Sigmund Freud and several others, was a founding member — and first president — of the famed and original Vienna Psychoanalytic Society. He is regularly mentioned along with Freud and Carl Jung (not a member of the Vienna group) as a leading theorist of what came to be called "depth psychology," or the effort to discover whatever could be found to underlie and account for behaviors that otherwise and in themselves were not readily understandable.

Of these three pioneers, Adler was the most attentive to the social context of each unique pattern of individual subjectivity, and of any particular expression of discouragement. He was therefore the most confident of the three about the resources for correction and cure of psychic distress to be found both in empathic understanding and in the improvements in social conditions made possible by education and public health initiatives. He was especially alert to the suffering brought about by notions of social inequality. In ways strikingly ahead of many, including many in the professional class of his time, he recognized and exposed the deleterious effects of the fears of humiliation or subordination associated with gender inequality and personal sexual identity, most notably the fears of being disregarded as "only a woman" or as "not man enough."

During the second half of the 20th Century Adler's distinctive optimism and his confident prescriptions for human improvement came under attack as "superficial" and "unrealistic." That this happened will be understood by consideration of its context: the appalling legacy of two World Wars, and the incomparable atrocities and devastations associated with them. Add to these the widespread conflicts and genocides subsequent to World War II that have marked the struggles to replace colonial rule, then coming to an end, with the establishment of new political structures of national independence. It can seem inevitable that Adler's contributions to psychological understanding would be dismissed in this atmosphere of more pessimistic assessments of the supposed determinants and frightening potential of human behavior.

But the rejection was not universal. A number of Adler's students, in psychiatry and (more widely influential) in education, followed his lead in theory and practice to great effect.

Oddly enough, disparagement and disdain of Adler on the one hand, and the effectiveness and influence of Adlerian theory on the other, led to many of his ideas being better recognized and remembered than he himself was. As an ironic example, consider Adler's terms, *inferiority feelings* and *inferiority complex.* They are representative of the strong divergence of opinion and the bitter dispute that disrupted and divided the original Vienna Psychoanalytic Society in 1911, ending with Adler's resignation from its presidency. Freud disliked such language for its being subjective and symbolic, and therefore not congenial to his conjectures about fixed and universal organic *drives* forging the elements of behavior in the heated chemistry of bodily cravings. However, when Freud died in 1939 his obituary in the *London Times* said, "Some of his terms have become part of everyday language, the inferiority complex, for example." The example was certainly a "part of everyday language," but it was as certainly not one of "his terms." Twenty-two years later the *New York Times* lent its authority to a fresh version of this misplacement of authorship in an obituary under the headline, "Dr. Karl [*sic*] Jung is dead . . . coined Introvert, Extrovert and Inferiority Complex." Those misapplications of authorship doubtless annoyed (perhaps also amused) many of Adler's friends and students, but that has not been the end of it.

Some muddles have a way of persisting, and this one has done as much as any other to distract the world of learned intellectual discourse from a serious appreciation of the importance of Adler's contributions to our understanding of ourselves. In an essay in the Sunday Magazine of the *New York Times* for April 14, 2006, Josef Joffe, publisher-editor of the German weekly *Die Zeit*, reflected on European resentments of American cultural influences as expressed in disparagements of the latter as "vulgar, inauthentic or stolen." Joffe concluded by saying, "If we could consult Dr. Freud, he would take a deep drag on his cigar and pontificate about inferiority feelings being compensated by hauteur and denigration." Although this is among the least likely of the things Freud might say if we could consult him on any subject, Joffe's error is a sign of something that continues to characterize memories of Adler and Freud and their important differences, something we feel called upon to correct.

It is clear that the value of Adler's ideas has been better recognized than their origins or the name of their author. In Freud's case, it is the other way around: His name remains a talisman, even as the applicability and implications of his ideas are less and less credited and more and more set aside as misleading, even destructive, and as attempts are made to salvage the value of his theory by ascribing Adler's accomplishments to his credit. If it is not already too late, it is high time to sort things out.

The task is daunting. Prejudices are deeply entrenched, and guidance is often faulty. On one occasion, when challenged to account for something someone claimed to have learned from him, Adler pointed to our present difficulty when he famously said, "I do not choose my followers; they choose me." And, as it is certainly fair to add, even his most devoted followers did not always understand all that was included in or implied by his way of studying human beings and human being. Adler was not an Adlerian, obviously, and we should expect that not all those who think of themselves as following him will agree with him or with each other on every or any point. To complicate matters, he often taught with what some have described as a careless, even reckless disregard for the systematic development of a coherent body of literature.

As time passes, however, Adler's writings, and the transcriptions of his lectures, are better and better edited and organized. Further, his ideas are increasingly expanded into the writings of others who defer to his authority. It has seemed important to us, therefore, to work toward some common understanding of the meanings and implications of the terms he employed, and so to contribute to a more coherent discussion of his work among those who are drawn to study it.

What's in a name?

— Shakespeare

This is the rhetorical question put by Juliet, everyone's favorite 14-year-old heroine. Her answer has all the unarguable certainty that accompanies the intoxicated feelings of a young person in the turbulence of her first love:

> *That which we call a rose*
> *By any other word would smell as sweet.*

Yes. However, as older people are irritatingly likely to say to young persons in this developmental phase, scarcely anyone will know what you are referring to if you call it by "any" other word. Names are not arbitrary matters; their effective use has nothing to do with an individual's preference or caprice. If, instead of saying, "Eat your vegetables," we were to say, "Eat your pajamas," the command would have a diminished force (making it even less likely to be obeyed than it usually is).

Our point here is that names and words, and language itself, are both achievements and facilitators of the cooperative arrangements that enable us to maintain our lives in their social contexts. Each human community, and each of the varied patterns of social living, evolved along with a way of speaking in a language that was its own. Familiarity (from *family*), and the affection that it carries with it, have served to connect us in the words we use, the phrases in which we shape them, and the songs we sing or the stories we tell. Small wonder that people resist the extinction of their ways of speaking, even when the submersion of local dialect or the loss of a whole language is shown to be inevitable. Young people everywhere are moving to their futures by moving away from their parents' tongues, especially as they adopt the common forms of English now spreading around the globe. The old languages of many small communities are being forgotten, crowded out of use, much as the rush of change and the alteration of environments are extinguishing myriad animal and plant species. "No problem" is a phrase whose meaning is understood almost everywhere, even where that meaning is recognized as an empty gesture of reassurance. English is to languages as monoculture is to biodiversity, and as worrisome to some in its weed-like choking of local and unique forms of expression.

At the same time as this commonality is establishing itself, separate vocabularies of jargon multiply and persist, each reflecting a pattern of values, a body of conviction, or an area of special expertise. Whether published (as in the case of this present volume) or informally maintained, each may be said to have its own lexicon. An ideology dictates choices of words specific to itself, and so do each of the schools of thought in economics, political theory, or psychology by which we are currently seeking to understand ourselves.

This effort — to understand ourselves — is in itself a tax upon our understanding. That we are strangers to ourselves must often strike us as strange; we feel as if we are immediate to ourselves and therefore immune to misunderstanding what intuition discloses to us. But it is not so. We are unable to observe, directly, our way of observing, or how our observations themselves are shaped by what we value, what we fear, and what we desire.

Psychology is therefore an inherently difficult study, and those who enter upon it differ as to its proper subject matter, its proper method, and the proper understanding of its findings and their implications. Psychologists are regularly embarrassed by these differences. As a consequence there are recurrent attempts amongst us to establish our work on strict and unarguably scientific modes of measurement, usually thought to entail close examination of modulations in certain physical tissues and electrochemical processes concurrent with reported or observed fluctuations in thought patterns or emotional states. Variations in brain structure and function are ever more closely studied in the search for anomalies that may be correlated to behaviors that are also regarded as anomalous, thereby to eliminate ambiguity and uncertainty from psychology. So far the results of these studies have not prevented an enlargement of the field of disputes.

We psychologists need not reproach ourselves, or each other, for our inexactitudes. Even in considering our physical world human beings are without a cosmic vantage from which to perceive directly our situation in the universe, or the universe itself. We conceive of our situation by means of models and images into which our present sense of the facts may be seen to fit.

Until recently (that is, until a few short centuries ago), we were still thinking of ourselves as if we were at the center of a great whirling sequence of spheres revolving around our stable earth in predictable cycles and epicycles. Galileo, Copernicus, and Newton first challenged and began to correct that conception, and we are all still learning to think in ways their discoveries opened to us. But that learning is not complete. The Ptolemaic schema they overturned still shapes our common sense of sunrise and sunset, and is still more useful to sailors (when navigating without electronic guidance) than is the new and scientifically more compelling one. It has been, in some analogous ways, the same in psychology.

As this field of study began to define itself, psychologists were like the astronomers who had no point of vantage outside the solar system from which to examine that system. We had no vantage outside the field of human phenomena from which to study those phenomena. We were unable to gain a perception of the human field in which we ourselves with our interests and biases inhered. Our efforts played their part in the shaping of our study; we were working to form better conceptions of ourselves by which to test hypotheses and construct patterns for understanding ourselves. The behaviors of domesticated animals were considered for models (carrot and stick), and the fixed action patterns of the wild creatures intrigued us. Further, we wanted to establish ourselves as scientists in an era in which mechanical ideas of matter in motion represented an imposing authority that governed assumptions. The dynamics of the steam engine, traced in heat and pressure and energy either released or exploding in violence was a rich mine of images for psychic pressure and the desire for release of tension. The phenomena of electromagnetism, providing unprecedented resources of power for the accomplishment of human enterprises, had unmistakable effects upon the analogies by which to describe ourselves as dynamos in our restless exertions and blind exercises of power.

As a physician, examining persons living under the stress of injuries, illnesses, anomalies, or social handicaps, Adler did not limit himself to these mechanistic assumptions of early scientific thought. As a healer, he was considering the strategies of impaired persons and was struck by the various ways individuals move to compensate for their disadvantages in the struggle to go on with their lives. He observed them persisting in efforts to recover and maintain balance, adapting their behaviors with whatever resources remained available to them, however diminished, to meet the requirements of their situations. Many early psychologists were embarrassed by the common-sense terms Adler employed in his examinations of sick people, terms suggesting purpose or goals. They wanted scientific psychology to limit inquiry into what *made* people act as they did, what *determined* behavior, or what *impressed* itself upon the individual in his or her development and *caused* the consequent variables of character. Many observers of human life sound as if they want to retain these limitations even now.

This is changing. Psychologists are beginning to incorporate the new possibilities for understanding opened to us by quantum theory in physics and epigenetics in biology. As they locate their work in the context of evolutionary thinking, psychologists are more and more informed by examination of the ways in which, in line with the need to adapt to environmental challenge, individuals move as members of whole groups in making use of environmental opportunity. To a student of Adler these developments are signs of confirmation of his fundamental and enduring contributions. However, until the field of psychology is more settled, and our several ways of making sense of ourselves are more clearly in harmony with one another, Adlerians are likely to continue to think of themselves, and to be thought of, as distinguished from other theorists by their particular school of thought.

The will to power.

— Nietzsche

It would be hard to identify a phrase more fraught with troublesome consequence for Adler than *the will to power*. Originally Adler thought he had found in it a dramatic description for the centerline of human striving, and perhaps for the striving of all living beings. Those who are sympathetic to his way of attending to *movement* will understand his reaching to adopt a phrase so marked by vitality as this one. The words were not his own however, and Adler was unable to use them without inviting associations that were directly contrary to his intentions. In summaries of his ideas current to this day, these associations continue to deflect understanding of his purpose. Who has not heard, in comparisons of the two men, that Freud studied the importance of sex, while Adler emphasized the importance of power? Few have had the leisure to inquire beyond this distinction. Even among those who have inquired further, many thought Freud to be the more compelling of the two. Sex seemed to them more obviously universal in its operations, and more fascinating in its functioning, as well as more mysteriously tangled in its attendant disturbances than could anything thought of in connection with the more abstract image of power.

Power has not had a second place in the larger world of discourse outside psychology however. In economic and social theory Karl Marx (1818-1883) is still studied, and it appears likely that he will continue to be studied for many more years. (Also likely is that this study will be more profitable the more Marx's thinking is distinguished from the later notions and practices of Lenin, Stalin, Mao, and Pol Pot.)* More arresting for our present purpose, if more difficult to appreciate, is Friedrich Nietzsche (1844-1900), whose challenges to the accepted assumptions of 19th Century European society were as influential as they were (often) regarded as reprehensible. In brief, Nietzsche argued that mass society was producing a shrunken form of humanity, hemmed in by custom and limited by a morality of deference to others. He called for a new birth of humanity in pursuit of a new ideal of mastery, freedom, and self-assertion. The will to power would guide these super men toward new heights of achievement and joy. It was an imagery that appealed to idealistic reformers and radical revolutionaries. After Nietzsche's death, and in distorted forms alien to his thinking, the notion of a will to power helped prepare the ground for the seductions of Nazism and the crimes of Hitler.

For Adler *the will to power* was a phrase seemingly tailor-made to describe *both* the self-created goal of striving toward success *and* the basic (and perhaps most common) error to which we are vulnerable in the course of that striving, namely the will to dominate or out-do others. Being, as we are at every moment, in the course of a development, we first reach an awareness of ourselves at a time in which we are no longer as weak and ignorant and dependent on others as we were as infants, and still not as strong and knowledgeable and independent as we hope to become. This initial impression of being in an incomplete stage of development contributes to the template we carry for all our succeeding judgments of ourselves. The problems of life as they arise continually challenge our developing (or diminishing) sense of adequacy. Even when our courage and optimism prepare us to meet these problems, we may persist in a feeling that our ability to solve and overcome their attendant difficulties is being put to the test as we address them. Small wonder, then, that we are so given to envisioning ourselves idealized, *as we would be* if we were not limited, threatened with defeat, or unsure of the outcome of our efforts. The appeal of the comic book hero Superman shows how much charm there is in such imagery. (For more adult reflection, Nietzsche's ideal was soon satirized by George Bernard Shaw in his play, *Man and Superman*, where the intellectual hero's fine pretenses to personal superiority are brought to

---

*Although each of these four claimed Marx as authority for his rationale of despotism, it can be argued that they were all in fact more truly the historical heirs of Cromwell and the righteous savagery of the 17th Century Puritan revolution in England.

ground by the *life force* — a favorite Shavian idea — expressed through the woman who decides he will marry her.)

Harder to see in ideas of superiority and power (except in the monstrous behavior of absolute tyrants) is the destructive counterpart included in them, namely their demand that everyone else but the super one be content (or be forced) to accept relative positions of inferiority and subordination. Adler saw that this part of the self-ideal, being so far from the common sense of social living, must necessarily be veiled. For all those not in the grotesque positions of tyrants, the demand for the submission of others can be stated only indirectly. Being unclear (or, unspeakable!) even to the conscience of those who press the demand, it is allowed (in fact it is required) to remain outside of consciousness, in the realm of the un-understood.

> *Words are too awful an instrument for good*
> *and evil to be trifled with: they hold above*
> *all other powers a dominion over thoughts.*
>
> — *Wordsworth*

Adler frequently spoke as one who would have appreciated the importance of this warning. He once said that we must stop using the phrase "the opposite sex," because it introduces the idea of opposition into discussions of sexuality, the one aspect of our lives that depends most plainly upon cooperation for its successful exercise. This was long before the revived Feminist Movement of the latter half of the 20th Century instructed us all on the subject of consciousness-raising through the deliberate alteration of common ways of speaking. As we have seen regarding *the will to power*, however, Adler's consciousness did not in this instance protect him from the trouble that haunted him and haunts his successors to this day as a result of his attempt to make Nietzsche's fighting words serve his own encouraging purposes. He tried to escape the trouble by arguing that he had meant to use the phrase only to describe pathology, not healthy striving, but the damage had been done.

Another German term, *Lebenstil*, most often translated into English as *lifestyle*, is a further borrowing, from another theorist, working in a quite different stream of intellectual investigation. Max Weber (1864-1920), a founder of modern sociology, coined the term to describe a pattern of tastes and behaviors distinctive of a social class. One of Weber's students introduced it to Adler as perhaps preferable to the term, *life plan*, which Adler had been using to describe the way one develops a unique character in pursuing a personal guiding image of success. As Adler conjured him in a didactic image, there is one private soldier indistinguishable from all the others in a line of march, who knows what the others do not know, namely, that at the bottom of his pack, hidden under all his other gear, is a field marshal's baton. Adler drew this picture to express the sense of the guiding line of a secret ambition, hidden from all, but secure in the self-image of the individual, and directed toward a particular and concrete goal of triumph over feelings of inferiority.

The trouble with Adler's image (and the term *life plan*) was how easily it could be reified, that is, mistaken as limited to the description of a real and particular soldier with a real and hidden baton. The word *lifestyle* has about it the advantage of a connotation more elusive and encompassing than the word, *plan.* The notion of style, suggestive of the work of the creative artist, could also draw upon the common experiences of discerning a person's individuality in his or her actions, as, for example, in the recognition of a distinctive style in handwriting (once referred to by Adler as "frozen movement"). *Lifestyle* is certainly a term more difficult to reify than *life plan.* On the other hand, and especially in its Standard English translation from the German, *Lebenstil*, it does not carry as strong a connotation of movement toward a goal. (*Livingstyle* would be more literal, and would extend to include the desired sense of direction and vitality, but it would also be more arch and less at home in English idiom.)

The term *lifestyle* has in it another unfortunate distraction from Adler's purposes in that it continues in use as it originated with Max Weber, namely, in descriptions of the patterns that characterize the distinguishing behaviors of people in various groups and social classes. Further reduced from the seriousness of sociology, and remote from the purposes of psychological study, the term has also come to connote tastes and preferences in interior design, salad dressings, and vacation resorts, as reported on in the "Life Style" section of many a Sunday newspaper.

In retrospect, even when all these misleading associations are noted, and when we reflect on the fruitful use to which Adler put the term *lifestyle,* it remains hard to think how he could have found a better term to denote the distinctive way persons move in thought, and affect, and bodily activity to express their several senses of what is open to them for advancement and achievement.

Language must continually be remade
if it is to reflect reality.

— *Brad Leithauser*

If this imperative of a former Poet Laureate of the United States has authority, a day may come when all the terms in this present collection will be seen as outmoded and in need of replacement. Until then our present task is limited to the clarification that comes from careful definition, regular allusion to context, and (what is most difficult) faithful translation.

Consider, as an example, a short historical review of the meaning and use of the term, *Individual Psychology*. To start at the end, this is the term still sometimes used to distinguish Adler's theoretical orientation, but note that we are already in a struggle here, revealed by the word *sometimes*. In fact the term, *Individual Psychology*, is less and less used outside academic circles. *Adlerian Psychology*, or just *Adlerian*, is taking its place. (The title of this book gives the example.)

Why is this? If Adler's own choice was Individual Psychology, why won't Adler's followers use it? Well, to start at the beginning, Adler's own choice was another word, a German one: *Individualpsychologie*. It looks as if the German word were the same as the English phrase, even if pronounced differently. The two-word English term, however, has connotations and suggestions that are quite different from the one-word German term, and so it can fairly be said that this apparently direct translation obscures, even misrepresents the original. In English, *Individual Psychology* immediately suggests the psychological study of individuals or an individual as distinct from a psychological study of groups. In this it certainly catches one nuance of the German word, pointing to the consideration of uniqueness in what Adler liked to say was "the individual variant" apart from any general pattern of human thought and behavior. But there is more. Adler's German word includes the concept of the *indivisibility* of the person as an organic unity who is, further, to be understood as wholly and *indivisibly* embedded in a historical and social context. (We have more to say about this in the text that follows.)

This is a small example of the difficulties encountered in moving from one language to another. Words have histories, and carry memories, and resonate with the echoes of their different uses. The combinations of these things can be unique in each instance of use. To carry words from one language to another is almost always to carry some shades of addition or subtraction with them, frequently unnoticed.

Larger examples of these difficulties can be found in the terms *inferiority feeling* and *community feeling*. Any serious student of Individual Psychology must be able to appreciate the importance of these terms for an understanding of Adler's theory. The *inferiority feeling*, though it can't be said to be an exact replica, is a rather straightforward representation in English of Adler's German word, *Minderwertigkeitsgefühl*. As for *community feeling*, there is no general agreement about its being the correct translation of Adler's *Gemeinschaftsgefühl.* Adler allowed himself to be convinced that *social interest* — a term used to mean an interest in the interests of others — would do well enough; consequently this term has come to enjoy wide currency. As reinforcement, Adler then took up retranslating it back into German, as *Soziale Interesse*, a term with associations to Karl Marx and Friedrich Engels, who used it in their book, "The Holy Family," where they say, "If correctly understood, 'interest' is the basis of all morality. The issue is, to make one's private interest coincide or be in harmony with social interest, interest in mankind."

We have reasons to think that this shift from *feeling* to *interest* is regrettable, and that private interest does inhere in the community feeling, and does not have to be *made* to fit there. We expand upon these reasons further on in this text in what may seem like a Quixotic tilting at a windmill of usage. Here we will say, in brief, that when Adlerians talk about *social interest* they too often seem to be indulging in a moralistic commendation of a hazily defined virtue, thereby trivializing the meaning of *Gemeinschaftsgefühl* and missing the critical importance originally placed upon it.

As Adler developed his schema for understanding the human data presented to him, his use of the terms *community feeling* and *inferiority feeling* referred to capacities he understood to be as uniquely developed in the human species as are language and the upright gait. For Adler, these primary and ineluctable feelings (where they are not denied, undeveloped, misunderstood, or otherwise deformed and misdirected) make it possible for us to assess correctly our situation in the world. They are therefore to be understood as apertures of awareness into a primary reality, the reality of our existential situation, independent of subjective opinion and bias. We *feel* (and we are!) frail, partial, fallible and mortal; we *are* (and we feel ourselves to be!) parts of a larger whole in which what we choose to do shapes the whole for better or worse. Our capacity for cultivating the art of human being is to be found in these fundamental feelings. Out of them we construct our responses to the command to love our neighbors as ourselves. This is a capacity. It must be cultivated, and its only chance to be cultivated is in a community that cherishes its possibility. And the chance may be missed.

That word startled my soul, and it awoke, full

of the spirit of the morning, full of joyous, exultant

song. Until that day my mind had been like a

darkened chamber, waiting for words to enter and

light the lamp, which is thought.

> — *Helen Keller*, describing her experience, as
> Anne Sullivan spelled the word, *water*, into her hand.

This book comes with our hope that it will contribute to lighting the lamp of clear and useful thought about the human experience of human being. It contains words and our reflections on words — words Adler sometimes coined, and words he sometimes borrowed. He left these words to stand as emblematic of his unsparing understanding of psychic error, folly, and suffering, his prescriptions for the correction and mitigation of these unavoidable human shortcomings, together with his optimistic assumptions of the human reality as it has emerged and is emerging from the cosmic reality of evolution and the history of our development. *The Lexicon* provides a vocabulary by which to think about thinking as a dimension of movement, and to do so in ways that neither flatter vanity nor undermine courage. It also includes words and phrases bearing meanings Adler noted for specific rejection. Finally, it includes terms and phrases used by those who, following his lead, made and are making contributions to the continuing development and applications of his theory.

At this juncture, it is a work in progress. At some point we must let the text go to press unfinished, expecting that other terms will come to our attention as a consequence of its appearance. Your comments will help in that regard, and we look forward to receiving them.

Robert L. Powers

ADLERIAN PSYCHOTHERAPY

The Individual Psychology of Alfred Adler (Adler, 1964a) contains, in excerpts throughout the text, accounts of Adler's techniques of **psychotherapy**, or ways of UNDERSTANDING and treating the patient. Especially relevant is Chapter 13 (pp. 326-349), the Introduction, "UNDERSTANDING the Patient," "Explaining the Patient to Himself," "The Therapeutic Relationship," and "Special Aspects and Techniques of Treatment." Similarly, there are valuable examples of UNDERSTANDING and treating the patient throughout *Superiority and Social Interest* (Adler, 1979). Also pertinent is Part III: "Case Interpretation and Treatment" (pp. 139-201), the Introduction, "Two Grade-School Girls," "The Case of Mrs. A.," and "Technique of Treatment."

Rudolf Dreikurs (1973) systematized Adler's work by identifying four phases of **psychotherapy**: (a) rapport, or establishing and maintaining the therapeutic relationship; (b) investigation of the client's past and present life situations and the client's LIFESTYLE; (c) interpretations and the development of client self- UNDERSTANDING; and (d) reorientation. The "phases" are not set in a temporal sequence; they proceed in a logical order of primacy and dependency that pertains throughout the therapeutic encounter. By "rapport" is meant the ALIGNMENT OF GOALS of client and therapist. [See PSYCHOCLARITY/UNDERSTANDING; LIFESTYLE/LIFE-STYLE/STYLE OF LIVING/ STYLE OF LIFE; EXOGENOUS FACTOR.]

> From the very beginning the consultant must try to make CLEAR that the responsibility for his cure is the patient's business. . . . The adviser can only point out the MISTAKES, it is the patient who must make the truth living (p. 336).

> The most trustworthy approaches to the exploration of personality are given in a comprehensive UNDERSTANDING of (1) the earliest of childhood memories [EARLY RECOLLECTIONS], (2) the position of the BIRTH ORDER, (3) childhood disorders [ORGAN INFERIORITY; OVERBURDENING CHILDHOOD SITUATIONS], (4) day and night DREAMS, and (5) the nature of the EXOGENOUS FACTOR (pp. 327-328).

> [The client's] APPERCEPTION-schema must always be traced and unmasked as being immature and untenable, but suited to the purpose of continued fighting (p. 333).

> A real explanation must be so CLEAR that the patient knows and feels his own experience instantly (p. 335).

> The increased insight into himself then stands like a guardian over the patient and forces him to find more USEFUL paths for his desire to be above, and to dampen his DEPRECIATION TENDENCY (p. 357).

> In practice we attempt to undo the great ERRORS, to substitute smaller ERRORS, and to reduce these further until they are no longer harmful (p. 187).

> The cure or reorientation is brought about by a correction of the faulty picture of the world and the unequivocal acceptance of a mature picture of the world (p. 333).

> Nobody who has understood anything of INDIVIDUAL PSYCHOLOGY would attempt to cure by upbraiding the patient, as if we could do good by taking up a moralistic attitude. A patient has to be brought into such a state of FEELING that he likes to listen, and wants to UNDERSTAND. Only then can he be influenced to live what he has understood (p. 335).

> In every step of treatment we must not deviate from the path of ENCOURAGEMENT (p. 342).

ADOLESCENCE

For some children, the challenges of **adolescence** are too great. Adler listed **adolescence** among common EXOGENOUS FACTORS precipitating psychological disturbances and maladaptations, since adolescence "provides the child with new situations and new tests . . . [where] mistakes in his STYLE OF LIFE may reveal themselves which were hitherto unobserved" (p. 439). Children who have been TRAINED and SELF-TRAINED to be COOPERATORS and CONTRIBUTORS may be "stimulated by their new freedom" and may "see the road towards fulfillment of their ambitions clear before them" (p. 440). Others, who are less well prepared to take advantage of this step toward adult responsibilities, will become DISCOURAGED at this point in their development, thinking less of the satisfactions to be won than of the threat of failure implicit in the idea of falling short of their GOALS. [See MISTAKEN GOALS OF THE DISCOURAGED CHILD.]

A great portion of responsibility for the success or failure of young people in their socio-sexual adaptations resides in the ENCOURAGEMENT (or lack of it) they receive from parents and other teachers.

> The **adolescent** may be understood as having the body of an adult and the status of a child (Dreikurs, personal communication, n.d.)

> **Adolescence** means one thing above all else: [The individual] must prove that he is no longer a child (p. 439).

> All the dangers of **adolescence** come from a lack of proper TRAINING and equipment for the three problems of life [the LIFE TASKS of community, occupation, and love] (p. 439).

> The means to combat . . . harmful [SEXUAL] influences are: preparation of children for their role as fellow men, clarification of their SEXUAL role at an early age, and friendly relations with their PARENTS (p. 443).

> The problem of the so-called natural development of SEXUALITY is not as simple as psychoanalysis teaches. . . . Keep in mind that no childhood offense is considered as serious and punished as severely than development toward the sexual norm. For boys . . . it is much easier to turn through mutual masturbation to homosexuality than to turn to normal sexual behavior. [Normal heterosexual intercourse] is much more strictly forbidden and is usually so severely punished that, in view of the dangers connected with it, the early-maturing youngsters are deterred from the other sex. Obviously, these early signs are inadequate evidence of innate homosexuality. There is immeasurable horror when a child behaves in the normal SEXUAL way. Thus what we observe in children again and again must be regarded as influenced by external circumstances. We do not know what development SEXUALITY would take if we would not, and would not have to, set up barriers against it (Adler, 1978, p. 365).

> **Adolescence** is, for INDIVIDUAL PSYCHOLOGY, simply a stage of development. . . . We do not believe that any stage of development, or any situation can change a person. But it does act as a test (Adler, 1930, p. 209).

See Walton, F. X. (1980) and Dinkmeyer, D. & McKay, G. D. (1998) for discussions of further MISTAKEN GOALS of discouraged adolescents: Excitement, Peer Acceptance, and Superiority.

AGGRESSION DRIVE

H. L. and R. R. Ansbacher state that Adler "introduced the concept of an **aggression drive**" in 1908, but that he later "subsumed **aggression** under the larger concept of STRIVING for overcoming, where **aggression** is but one of the forms this STRIVING may take" (p. 267). Adler was, in 1908, still a member of the Freudian circle, shaping his thought in terms congruent with drive psychology, and already searching for "a unifying dynamic principle" (p. 34). Adler continued to use the term **aggression**, but, after considering it as the form of the "confluence of drives" (p. 34) that he postulated on his way toward a HOLISTIC theory, he came to see it not as a "**drive**" at all, but as only one of an illimitable number of manifestations of the STRIVING for SUPERIORITY and, ultimately, perfection.

> "I enriched psychoanalysis," Adler told his friends with a grim smile, "by the **aggressive drive**. I gladly make them a present of it" (Bottome, 1939, p. 64).

ALIGNMENT OF GOALS vs. RESISTANCE

INDIVIDUAL PSYCHOLOGY promotes relationships of mutual respect between doctor and patient, therapist and client. Adler took the patient off the psychoanalytic couch and invited him or her to take a chair like his own. This set the stage for a discussion between two persons of equal worth, trying to solve a problem together. He emphasized the importance of **aligning** doctor-patient **goals**. It is the responsibility of the doctor to rethink his approach to close the gap between the patient's ambitions and the doctor's responsibility if the doctor offers certain explanations of the patient's movement not congenial to the patient, or makes requests for certain behaviors that are not welcomed by the patient. It is the doctor's task to educate the patient for COOPERATION, an impossible undertaking if the two parties are not engaged in the same problem-solving effort. **Resistance,** a term arising in psychoanalysis, relates to the Freudian concept of repression, so is not compatible with Adlerian theory, which discounts the notion of repression. Adler observed that the therapist must be alert to the DEPRECIATION TENDENCY that is invariably present among those who have failed to meet the tasks of life successfully because they have not learned to COOPERATE.

> The proper therapeutic relationship, as we understand it . . . [requires] a relationship of mutual trust and respect. This is more than mere establishment of contact and rapport. Therapeutic COOPERATION requires an **alignment of goals**. When the **goals** and interests of the patient and therapist clash, no satisfactory relationship can be established. Winning the patient's COOPERATION for the common task is a prerequisite for any therapy; maintaining it requires constant vigilance. What appears as "**resistance**" constitutes a discrepancy between the **goals** of the therapist and those of the patient. In each case, the proper relationship has to be re-established, differences solved, and agreement reached (Dreikurs, 1973, p.7).

> It is the DEPRECIATION TENDENCY which underlies the phenomenon Freud described as **resistance** and erroneously understood as the consequence of the repression of sexual impulses (p. 337).

> Since the physician obstructs the NEUROTIC strivings of the patient, the physician is regarded as an obstacle, an obstruction, preventing the attainment of the superiority-ideal. . . . Therefore every patient will attempt to DEPRECIATE the physician, to deprive him of his influence, and to conceal from him the true state of affairs (p. 337).

> The so-called **resistance** is only lack of COURAGE to return to the USEFUL SIDE OF LIFE. This causes the patient to put up a defense against treatment, for fear that his relation with the psychologist should force him into some useful activity in which he will be defeated (p. 338).

ANTITHETICAL MODE OF APPERCEPTION

Used in the common parlance of psychological discourse in Adler's day, the term **antithetical mode of apperception** entered INDIVIDUAL PSYCHOLOGY in association with the BASIC MISTAKES or INTERFERING IDEAS of the LIFE-STYLE, commonly experienced as possibilities set in dialectical opposition, and weighing on the person as GOALS or imperatives. Adler used the phrase to identify the "sharply schematizing, strongly abstracting **mode of apperception**" of the NEUROTIC as "something like the debit and credit sides of bookkeeping . . . and admits no degrees in between" (p. 248). Although Adler sometimes used the image of polar opposites, he was not considering a range of degrees of separation between positive and negative evaluations, as was common in the work of Fritz Perls and some others. For Adler, the **antithetical mode of apperception** was to be understood by analogy to the difference between heads and tails in the toss of a coin. This accounts for the exaggerated efforts of discouraged persons to preserve their SELF-ESTEEM by claims to SUPERIORITY, since in the NEUROTIC logic failure to do so threatens a complete loss of human value or any claim to standing in the human COMMUNITY. Variations on the theme may insinuate (and attempt to disguise) claims to SUPERIORITY by wrapping them in morbid expressions of penitence, remorse, guilt, and worthlessness (for example, by those contending for the position "chief of sinners").

> The **apperception-schema** of the patient evaluates all impressions as if they were fundamental matters and dichotomizes them in a purposeful manner into above-below, victor-vanquished, masculine-feminine, nothing-everything, etc. (p. 333).

> The UNDERSTANDING of the world according to concrete pairs of opposites corresponds to the primitive attempts of the child to orient himself in the world and to SAFEGUARD himself. Among these pairs I have regularly found: (1) *above-below* and (2) *masculine-feminine* (p. 249).

APPERCEPTION/BIASED APPERCEPTION

Apperception refers to the personal values and interests determining the mode in which an individual perceives self, others, and the world. The mode of perceiving is biased by CONVICTIONS; thus, each individual has a **biased apperception** of both subjective and objective experience. The schema of **biased apperception** defines the individual's PHENOMENOLOGICAL FIELD.

[After the first four or five years of life] a well-determined SCHEMA OF APPERCEPTION (*Apperzeptionsschema*) is established, and the child's conclusions and actions are directed in full accord with the final [SELF-] IDEAL end form to which he aspires (pp. 181-182).

Perception can never be compared with a photographic apparatus; it always contains something of the individual's uniqueness. Not everything one sees is also perceived, and if one asks for the perceptions of two persons who have seen the same picture, one receives the most varied answers. The child perceives in his environment only that which . . . fits his previously formed uniqueness (p. 210).

What a person perceives, and how he does so, constitutes his particular uniqueness (p. 210).[1]

The child will not perceive given situations as they actually exist, but under the prejudice of his own interests (p. 189).

The world is seen through a stable schema of **apperception**: Experiences are interpreted before they are accepted, and the interpretation always accords with the original meaning given to life. Even if this meaning is very gravely mistaken, even if the approach to our problems and tasks brings us continually into misfortunes and agonies, it is never easily relinquished (p. 189).

People find it very difficult to free themselves from the schema into which they have grown during the first years of life (p. 190).

Denying the connection between the experience and the schema of **apperception** is like taking single notes out of a melody to examine them for their value and meaning (p. 183).

THE ARRANGEMENT

Adler named a section of *The Practice and Theory of Individual Psychology* (1959) "The '**Arrangement**' of the NEUROSIS" (p. 37). By this phrase Adler referred to the constructions created by the NEUROTIC person, those " '**arrangements**' lying along the path to the feeling of superiority" (Adler, 1959, p. 44). In an example, Adler notes the NEUROTIC who "would sing and hum to himself on the street at public places to show his contempt for the world (i.e., *he is arranging* feelings of superiority)" (Adler, 1959, p. 48).

> The hypnotic nature of the GOAL of the NEUROTIC forces his whole psychic life into an integrated adaptation. . . . The strong urge toward the integration of his personality . . . has been created by his tendency to SAFEGUARD himself. The path is made secure and unalterable by the proper schematic "**arrangements**" of character-traits, affect-preparations and symptoms (Adler, 1959, p. 38).

> DISCOURAGEMENT, the surest sign of a NEUROTIC, forces him to put distance between himself and absolutely necessary decisions. To justify this distance he resorts to **arrangements** which pile up in front of him like a mountain of junk (p. 305).

"AS IF" (FICTIONS)

As used in ADLERIAN PSYCHOLOGY, the phrase "**as if**" refers to both a basic philosophical construct and a psychotherapeutic technique.

As a philosophical construct, according to H. L. and R. R. Ansbacher (Adler, 1964), it was Hans Vaihinger's *The Philosophy of 'As If': A System of the Theoretical, Practical, and Religious Fictions of Mankind* (1911/1968) that provided Adler with the "philosophic foundation for his developing subjective [**fictional**] FINALISM (p. 78). And, "Vaihinger proposed that the individual's *activity* [L., *fictio*] of imaginative CREATING results in **fictions** that are (a) subjective, (b) CREATIVE, and (c) UNCONSCIOUS" (p. 90). Vaihinger (1968) states, "For us, the essential element in a **fiction** is not the fact of its being a conscious deviation from reality, a mere piece of imagination – but we stress the useful nature of this deviation. . . . Conceptual forms and **fictions** are expedient psychical constructs" (p. 99). [See SELF-IDEAL (*PERSÖNLICHKEITSIDEAL*).]

As a psychotherapeutic technique, therapists ask clients to behave "**as if**" a particular idea were true, that is, to *pretend* for an agreed-upon period or number of times, that a specific basic belief were *different*. For example, a single female client enters therapy complaining that she has no man in her life and suffers from loneliness. In a LIFESTYLE ASSESSMENT, it is uncovered that she has the notion that all men are untrustworthy. Holding this belief, she is afraid of them; consequently, she pushes them away by looking down on them and withholding friendship and affection. Using the "**as if**" technique, therapist and client agree that for one week (or one day, or one incident), the client will act "**as if**" it were true that men *are* trustworthy. The assumption of the "**as if**" technique is that when the client demonstrates respect for and places confidence in a man, she will begin to experience success, her negative bias will be undermined, new attitudes will begin to emerge, and her COURAGE and COMMUNITY FEELING fostered.

> The human mind shows an urge to capture into fixed forms through unreal assumptions, that is, **fictions**, that which is chaotic, always in flux, and incomprehensible. . . . [My task is] to advance this knowledge which I have gained from the psychological consideration of the NEUROSIS and PSYCHOSIS and which is found, according to the evidence of Vaihinger, in all scientific views (p. 96).

See Carich, M. S., 1997, for additional "**as if**" techniques.

BELONGING

The lectures and writings of Adler and Dreikurs demonstrate that while they agreed that the STRIVING FOR SUPERIORITY is universal, they disagreed as to the CONCRETIZATION of the GOAL of striving.

For Adler, the GOAL of SUPERIORITY STRIVING is always a fictional form of the idea of *perfection* (overcoming, mastery, fulfillment, completion), CONCRETIZED by the individual in the subjectively conceived PERSONALITY IDEAL, while for Dreikurs the GOAL of STRIVING is always CONCRETIZED in some image of **belonging**. B. H. Shulman reported that Dreikurs stated, in a medical school lecture, that he located his theoretical position as being midway between Adler and Karen Horney (Terner and Pew, 1978, p. 191). Horney (1945) believed that "a desire for '**belonging**' " (p. 50) is central to human motivation, and could have been the source of Dreikurs's thinking on this matter.

Adler did not locate his own position as midway between himself and Horney, and so did not envision the COMMUNITY FEELING as a GOAL; he postulated it as a human capacity, comparing it to the upright gait and the capacity for language, never completely absent, and always in need of cultivation. For Adler, MOVEMENT toward the GOAL of perfection (the PERSONALITY IDEAL), when it is individually and uniquely CONCRETIZED *on the USEFUL SIDE*, has its foundation in, and proceeds from, the **feeling of belongingness,** that is, the COMMUNITY FEELING (SOCIAL INTEREST). For Dreikurs, however, **belonging** is the GOAL of all striving, whether the individual's MOVEMENT is on the USEFUL or the USELESS SIDE of life.

H. L. Ansbacher (1985), the foremost Adlerian scholar, upon reading an assertion that "for Adler the strongest motivating force for the human being is the desire to **belong** to the social world," responded by saying "[If the writer] has a reference to Adler for this statement, I would like to know it. Rudolf Dreikurs often wrote of 'the need to **belong**' as the strongest motivating force and should be recognized as the author" (p. 7).

> Each individual tries to get himself accepted by the community. The desire to feel **belonging** to others is the fundamental motive in man (Dreikurs, 1949, p. 21).

> INDIVIDUAL PSYCHOLOGY stands firmly on the ground of EVOLUTION and, in the light of it, regards all human STRIVING as a STRIVING for perfection (p. 106).

> STRIVING towards a GOAL, towards an objective, we find everywhere in life. Everything grows "AS IF" it were STRIVING to overcome all imperfections and achieve perfection. This urge toward perfection we call the GOAL of overcoming, that is, the STRIVING to overcome (Adler, 1979, p. 86).

> The development of the child is increasingly permeated by the relationships of society to him. In time, the first signs of the innate SOCIAL INTEREST appear, the organically determined impulses of affection blossom forth, and lead the child to seek the proximity of adults. One can always observe that the child directs impulses of affection towards others and not towards himself, as Freud believes. These impulses vary in degree and differ with respect to different persons. In children over two years one can also see these differences in their verbal expressions. The **feeling of belongingness**, the **SOCIAL INTEREST**, takes root in the psyche of the child and leaves the individual only under the severest pathological changes of his mental life (p. 138).

> Feeling-at-home is an important part of SOCIAL INTEREST. The life on this poor crust of one who has SOCIAL INTEREST runs its course as though he were at home (p. 155).

THE BIG NUMBERS

The subjective field of perception is not limited to an extension in social space; it may include an extension in time, and especially in life-span. It appears that, in creating the GENDER GUIDING LINES, children regard their PARENTS as norms for what it means to be a man or a woman, and on the basis of these images they form expectations as to how life will be for them as they grow up. These expectations have to do with the way life unfolds over time. Powers and Griffith (1986) introduced the notion of **the big numbers** and observed that "the ages at which particular events took place in the life of a [person's] same-sex PARENT serve as 'markers' or points of reference, forming a private timetable against which to measure personal progress, for better or worse." As an example, they cited Paul A. Samuelson, the first American to receive the Nobel Prize in Economics, whose father died when Samuelson was twenty-three. After his father's death, Samuelson reported, "Consciously or unconsciously, I was a young man in a hurry because I felt that the limited lifespan of my male ancestors tolled the knell for me. What I was to do I would have to do early" (pp. 1, 6). [See GENDER GUIDING LINES AND ROLE MODELS.]

See Powers, R. L., & Griffith, J. (1992); Powers, R. L., Griffith, J., & Maybell, S. A. (1993).

COMMUNITY FEELING/SOCIAL FEELING/SOCIAL INTEREST

These are unsatisfactory English language translations of Adler's German term, *Gemeinschaftsgefühl*. Most accurate of these is **community feeling**, which encompasses the individual's awareness of BELONGING in the human community and the cosmos of which it is a part, and an UNDERSTANDING of his or her responsibility for the way the life of the community is being shaped by his or her actions. It is a fundamental sense of being one amongst the others as a fellow being. Adler, for whom English was a foreign language, allowed himself to be persuaded that the term, **social interest** (by which was meant an interest in the interests of others) could be used to express what Adler called "the action line of **community feeling**" (as cited in Ansbacher, 1992, p. 405), especially in relation to addressing the three LIFE TASKS. **Social feeling** has sometimes been used, but the term **social interest** eventually came to be preferred, perhaps to avoid association with the rhetoric of socialism or communism. **Community feeling/social interest,** regarded as a universal human capacity, must be cultivated and trained, and so is understood by analogy to the human capacity for language and speech. It is further thought of as an index to successful ADAPTATION (mental health): The more developed the **community feeling**, the more diminished the INFERIORITY FEELING with its associated sense of alienation and isolation; therefore, the effectiveness of psychotherapy or counseling depends upon increasing and strengthening the DISCOURAGED person's **community feeling** and **social interest**.

> A phrase which clearly expresses what we could contribute to an explanation [of **social interest** is]: "To see with the eyes of another, to hear with the ears of another, to feel with the heart of another" (p. 135).

> The capacity for identification, which alone makes us capable of friendship, LOVE of mankind, sympathy, occupation, and LOVE, is the basis of **social interest** and can be practiced and exercised only in conjunction with others (p. 136).

> [**Social interest** or **social feeling**] is more than a FEELING; it is an evaluative attitude toward life (p. 135).

> It means particularly the interest in, or the FEELING with, the community *sub specie aeternatatis* [under the aspect of eternity — Spinoza] (p. 142).

> Lack of **social interest**, always due to increased INFERIORITY FEELING, drives the individual into NEUROSIS or crime, and groups and nations toward the abyss of self-extermination (p. 449).

> **Social interest** is the true and inevitable COMPENSATION for all the natural weaknesses of individual human beings (p. 154).

> **Social interest** . . . is an innate potentiality which has to be consciously developed (p. 134).

> INDIVIDUAL PSYCHOLOGY maintains that the power of **social interest** lies at the basis of all social products, such as language and reason or "COMMON SENSE" (p. 449).

> Feeling-at-home is an immediate part of **social interest**. The life on this poor earth crust of one who has **social interest** runs its course as though he were at home (p. 155).

For a report and discussion of the *Sulliman Scale of Social Interest* (1973), see Oberst, U. E. & Stewart A. E. (2003), pp. 181-184.

COMPENSATION/OVER-COMPENSATION

In Adler's early experiences as a physician he began to use these terms to describe the phenomena of the MOVEMENT of living creatures, persisting in often heightened activity under the burden of a handicap, or the impairment of an organ; and the concomitant exaggerated, often superior development of another organ or organ system. Many of his patients came to him from the nearby Vienna Prater, an amusement park with circus features. Adler particularly noted the anxieties of acrobats and other performers concerning physical weakness or impairment and the corresponding attention they paid to self-care and physical training. He concluded that in response to a felt ORGAN INFERIORITY the organism as a whole moves to **compensate** for the particular organ weakness. This provided him with a bridge from the study of physical processes to an understanding of psychological processes.

In Adler's earliest medico-psychological text (*Study of Organ Inferiority and its Psychical Compensation*, 1907/1917), he referred to **compensatory** activity as mediated by what he termed the "psychical superstructure" (p. 41). Increasingly, as the effects of opinion and ambition — independent of organic structure — came clearer to him, he moved away from biological determinism, turning his attention to **compensation** tending toward **over-compensation** (exemplified in the classic story of Demosthenes, the stammerer who by dint of ambition and effort became a great orator). Considering the effect of cultural and societal biases and prejudices, especially as concerns ideas of masculine SUPERIORITY and feminine INFERIORITY, his thinking moved in a further fateful awareness, away from a strict physicalism toward social-psychological factors, and to the various ways individuals struggle to **compensate** for assumed ideas of INFERIORITY. He observed that the more pronounced the INFERIORITY FEELINGS, the more intense is the **compensatory striving**. This led to his further postulating that the only true **compensation** for such feelings is the development of COMMUNITY FEELING. [See FEMINISM; HISTORICAL CONTEXT: ADLER IN HIS TIME; MASCULINE PROTEST.]

> As in organic **compensation**, the effectiveness of psychological **compensation** is linked with increased activity and brings about striking, often superior and novel psychological phenomena (p. 98).

> The entire bearing, the identifying gestures, the play of children and their wishes, their DAY-DREAMS and favorite fairy tales, thoughts about their future occupational choice, all indicate that the **compensation tendency** is at work making preparations for the future role (p. 99).

> SOCIAL INTEREST [COMMUNITY FEELING] is the true and inevitable **compensation** for all the natural weaknesses of individual human beings (p. 154).

COMPULSION NEUROSIS/COUNTER-COMPULSION

According to H. L. and R. R. Ansbacher, Adler (1979) came to believe the **compulsion neurosis,** usually regarded as one of the several distinguishable patterns of NEUROTIC functioning, to be "apparently the prototype for all [NEUROSES]" (p. 112).

Adler (1979) observed that for the **compulsion neurotic** "one can always establish that there is a lack of preparation for the solution of the life problems and that this lack — whether it really exists or is 'believed' only in imagination — prevents him from advancing, so that he lapses into a HESITATING ATTITUDE . . . and turns to the secondary theater of operations." By this strategy he is "eliminating the **compulsion** of life by a **counter-compulsion**" (pp. 115-116).

Adler's UNIFIED THEORY of MENTAL ILLNESS (that MENTAL ILLNESS derives from faulty STYLES OF LIVING based on perceptual and conclusive ERRORS of the young child) supports a unified interpretation of all maladaptations as varieties of unique, individual, **counter-compulsive** RESISTANCE to the "**compulsion** of life," that is, to the demands of the community for COOPERATION and CONTRIBUTION in meeting THE TASKS OF LIFE.

> The **psychoneurosis** . . . has the ultimate purpose of SAFEGUARDING a person from a clash with his LIFE TASKS, that is, with reality, and of sparing him the danger of having the dark secret of his INFERIORITY revealed (p. 299).

> Nowhere does the mountain of SELF-ARRANGED difficulties become so obvious as in the **compulsion neuroses** (p. 305).

> The **compulsion neurotic** retires, so to speak, to a secondary field of action where he expends all his energies instead of devoting them to solving his primary problem (p. 305).

> Human nature generally answers external coercion with a countercoercion [**counter-compulsion**] (p. 457).

> The **compulsion** does not reside in the **compulsive** idea or action; it originates outside these, in the sphere of our normal social life. This is the source of the patient's NEUROTIC **compulsion** or urge. He must evade the realities of life, since he feels incompetent to face them. . . . He retreats farther and farther before the bayonets of life . . . [and makes] use of the motions that give him a feeling of complete SUPERIORITY (pp. 307-308).

13

CONCRETIZATION OF THE GOAL

The individual moves in the midst of life's demands in accordance with the FICTIONAL GOAL of the SELF-IDEAL, which must be made **concrete**. Adler observed that the healthy person uses his or her FICTION "to attain a **goal** in reality," while the NEUROTIC is "enmeshed" in his FICTION, unable to find his way "back to reality." At each step the **goal** is made **concrete**, to "capture into fixed forms" what exists in FICTIONS (p. 96). Adler likens the FICTION of the SELF-IDEAL to the FICTIONAL meridians and parallels we *use* (make **concrete**) for orientation. [See GOALS; GUIDING FICTION/FICTIONAL GOAL/FICITONAL FINALISM; SELF-IDEAL (*PERSÖNLICHKEITSIDEAL*).]

[The] **goal** must be made **concrete** to become clearer (p. 99).

[While the FICTIONAL GOAL remains constant] an individual may change . . . the way in which he makes his GOAL **concrete**. . . . The nearer to health and NORMALITY an individual is, the more he can find new openings for STRIVINGS when they are blocked in one particular direction. It is only the NEUROTIC who feels, of the **concrete** expressions of his **goal**, "I must have this or nothing" (p. 190).

The individual's artful construction of his form of life [LIFESTYLE] . . . follows by no means a causal process. The decisive factor is always the **concretized** FICTIONAL GOAL of life (p. 282).

A GOAL of OVERCOMING as an abstract formulation is unacceptable to the human mind. We need a more **concrete** formulation. Thus each individual arrives at a **concrete** GOAL of OVERCOMING through his CREATIVE POWER, which is identical with the self (p. 180).

CONSCIOUS/UNCONSCIOUS/UN-UNDERSTOOD

Adler departed from other theorists as concerns notions of "**the unconscious**," and "**consciousness**," arguing that "**the unconscious** is nothing other than that which we have been unable to formulate in clear concepts" (p. 232). He interpreted unknown motivation as material not yet understood ("**un-understood**") where UNDERSTANDING was not necessary to the individual's MOVEMENT. Included in this material are BASIC CONVICTIONS, biases, and GUIDELINES formed in early childhood, useful as a framework for preferences and ready choices, together with the fundamental orientation toward a personal GOAL of success. Adler's **un-understood** (an adjective) is to be contrasted to Freud's hypothesis of **the unconscious** (a noun), thought of as if a repository of reprehensible, and so inexpressible thoughts, impulses, and intentions that the "ego" guards against acknowledging. For Adler, **un-understood** material is consistent with the individual STYLE OF LIVING expressed in thought, feeling, and action.

> **The unconscious** is nothing other than that which we have been unable to formulate in clear concepts. It is not a matter of concepts hiding away in some **unconscious** or subconscious recesses of our minds, but of parts of our **consciousness**, the significance of which we have not fully understood (pp. 232-233).

> Where **consciousness** becomes necessary as a means of life, as a SAFEGUARD for the unity of the self and for the SELF-IDEAL, it will appear in the proper form and degree (p. 233).

> The biological significance of **consciousness** as well as **unconsciousness** rests in the fact that these states enable action according to a self-consistently oriented life plan [LIFE-STYLE] (p. 233).

> It is a general human phenomenon to lay aside thoughts which stand in our way, and take up those which advance our position. . . . That becomes **conscious** which advances us, and that remains **unconscious** which might disturb our argumentation (p. 233).

> Part of the mental life . . . operates "**unconsciously**" as some authors are wont to put it, or as we would say "**not understood**" (p. 192).

> The so-called **conscious** and **unconscious** are not contradictory, but form a single unity, and the methods used in interpreting the "**conscious**" life may be used in interpreting the "**unconscious**" or "**semi-conscious**" life, the life of our DREAMS (pp. 358-359).

CONTEXT PSYCHOLOGY vs. DEPTH PSYCHOLOGY

In the introduction to the original Basic Books edition of *The Individual Psychology of Alfred Adler* (Adler, 1956) the editors H. L. and R. R. Ansbacher state, "The INDIVIDUAL PSYCHOLOGY of Adler is first of all a **depth psychology**. By this is meant that part of dynamic psychology which goes beneath and beyond surface phenomena, taking UNCONSCIOUS motivation fully into account. For Adler, however, THE UNCONSCIOUS was not a separate category, but . . . merely that part of the subject's striving which he does not UNDERSTAND" (p. 3).

Eight years later, in the paperback Harper Torchbooks edition (Adler, 1964a) of the same text, they amended this passage as follows: "Adler's psychology was often called a **'depth' psychology**, that is, a psychology which discovers deeply buried **unconscious** phenomena. For Adler, however, THE UNCONSCIOUS was . . . merely that part of an individual's LIFE STYLE which he does not UNDERSTAND, and UNDERSTANDING is afforded by viewing all processes in their larger **context**. Therefore, one would better speak of Adler's psychology as **'context' psychology**" (p. 3). [See PSYCHOCLARITY/UNDERSTANDING.]

> INDIVIDUAL PSYCHOLOGY is far removed from all the presently declining theories of shallow **'depth psychology'** " (Adler, 1979, p. 99).

16

CONTRIBUTION

Contribution and COOPERATION are essential terms for the understanding of Adler's normative assessment of a person's MOVEMENT on the USEFUL SIDE of life. They refer to attitudes and actions that inhere in COMMUNITY FEELING/SOCIAL INTEREST and, as such, must be cultivated in children by their care-givers for the sake of their personal development as human beings as well as for the continuing development of the human race, of which they must UNDERSTAND themselves to be the guarantors.

> Life means — to **contribute** to the whole (p. 153).

> The only salvation from the continuously driving INFERIORITY FEELING is the knowledge and the FEELING of being valuable which originates from the **contribution** to the common welfare (p. 155).

> Every human being STRIVES for significance, but people always make MISTAKES if they do not see that their whole significance must consist in their **contributions** to the lives of others (p. 156).

> It is the STRIVING FOR SUPERIORITY which is behind every human creation and it is the source of all **contributions** which are made to our culture (p. 255).

COOPERATION

For Adler **cooperation** is the distinguishing characteristic of the successful human being. The formula we have used for teaching this is as follows: Human being is social being. Human problems are therefore social problems, requiring **cooperation** for their solution. Even so-called "personal" problems are, when unsolved, signs of the person's HESITATION or failure to engage **cooperatively** with others.

> All problems in our lives are social problems; and these can be solved only if we are interested in others (p. 411).

> Life presents only such problems as require [the] ability to **cooperate** for their solution (p. 136).

> The development of the innate potentiality for **cooperation** occurs first in the relationship of the child and mother (p. 135).

> The task of the mother is to turn the child as early as possible into a coworker (p. 373).

> [The pampered child's] interest was devoted to himself, and he never learned the use and necessity of **cooperation**. . . . [Grown-up pampered children are] on strike against **cooperating**, as ordinary human beings, in our ordinary human tasks (pp. 369-370).

> Psychotherapy is an exercise in **cooperation** and a test of **cooperation**. . . . We must work out [the patient's] attitudes and difficulties together. . . . We must **cooperate** with him in finding his MISTAKES, both for his own benefit and for the welfare of others (p. 340).

> All cases of failure which we have seen involve a lack of **cooperation.** Therefore **cooperation** between patient and consultant, as the first, serious, scientifically conducted attempt to raise SOCIAL INTEREST, is of paramount importance, and from the start all measures should be taken to promote the **cooperation** of the patient with the consultant (p. 340-341).

> All human judgments of value and success are founded, in the end, upon **cooperation**; this is the great shared commonplace of the human race (p. 255).

THE COURAGE TO BE IMPERFECT

The psychologist Sophie Lazarsfeld coined this phrase. According to H. L. Ansbacher's biographical note (Ansbacher, 1966, p. 152), Lazarsfeld was a therapist, writer, and Adlerian activist who joined the Vienna Individual Psychology Society after World War I. She first used the phrase in 1925 at the Second International Congress of Individual Psychology in Berlin. She later expanded on the idea, cautioning that "Adler viewed perfection as an ideal which can never really be reached," that there is a difference between "*sound* striving for perfection and the *NEUROTIC* wanting to be perfect [italics added]," and that in psychotherapy people "learn to face their own imperfection. . . . They acquire the **courage to be imperfect**" (Lazarsfeld, 1966, pp. 163-164).

According to Terner and Pew (1978), Dreikurs (having given proper credit to Lazarsfeld) popularized the phrase and it "came to be a leitmotif in his work" (p. 88). Dreikurs was concerned that perfectionism permeated the society and led to everyone's being mistake-centered rather than success-centered, focused on what people did wrong rather than what they did right. He concluded that since schools and enterprises of all kinds emphasize mistakes, the COURAGE of both children and adults is undermined until they lose confidence and HESITATE to act.

Terner and Pew (1978) cite as seminal a speech delivered by Dreikurs in 1970 at the University of Oregon in Eugene, excerpted below.

> To be human does not mean to be right, does not mean to be perfect. To be human means to be useful, to make contributions — not for oneself, but for others — to take what there is and to make the best of it. . . . We have to realize that we're good enough as we are; we never will be better, regardless of how much more we may know, how much more skill we may acquire, how much status or money or what-have-you. If we can't make peace with ourselves as we are, we never will be able to make peace with ourselves. This requires **the courage to be imperfect**; requires the realization that "I am no angel, that I am no superhuman, that I make mistakes, that I have faults. But I am pretty good because I don't *have* to be better than the others" — which is a tremendous relief. . . . If we learn to function — to do our best regardless of what it is — out of the enjoyment of the functioning, we can grow just as well, even better than if we drove ourselves to be perfect (p. 289).

COURAGE/ENCOURAGEMENT/DISCOURAGEMENT

Courage is here understood as the willingness to act in line with COMMUNITY FEELING (SOCIAL INTEREST) in any situation. It is fundamental to successful ADAPTATION. To **encourage** is to promote and activate the COMMUNITY FEELING, that is, the sense of BELONGING, value, worthwhileness, and welcome in the human community. As the loss of **courage**, or **discouragement**, is understood by INDIVIDUAL PSYCHOLOGY to be the basis of MISTAKEN and dysfunctional behavior, so **encouragement** is a major part of ADLERIAN PSYCHOTHERAPY and counseling.

The **discouraged** person has the same GOAL as the person with **courage**: to triumph over the INFERIORITY FEELING and to be seen as successful and worthy of respect in the human world. However, he or she lacks the **courage** to operate on the USEFUL SIDE OF LIFE, in the fear of being exposed as deficient. The MOVEMENT toward success is then deflected toward finding a place of personal SUPERIORITY *over* others, a MOVEMENT on the USELESS SIDE, marked by pretense, evasion, DISTANCE, and posturing in NEUROTIC, SOCIOPATHIC, or PSYCHOTIC processes and operations.

> The aim of INDIVIDUAL PSYCHOLOGY treatment is always to increase an individual's **courage** to meet the problems of life (p. 362).

> **Courage** is but one side of SOCIAL INTEREST (p. 342).

> We can understand by **courage** one side of COOPERATION (p. 437).

> Only the activity of an individual who plays the game, COOPERATES, and shares in life can be designated as **courage** (p. 166).

> In every step of the treatment, we must not deviate from the path of **encouragement**. This is in accordance with the conviction of INDIVIDUAL PSYCHOLOGY, by which so much untenable vanity feels offended, that "everybody can do everything" with the exception of amazingly high achievement, about the structure of which we cannot say very much anyway (p. 342).

> NEUROSIS and PSYCHOSIS are modes of expression for human beings who have lost **courage** (p. 343).

> All mistaken answers [to the TASKS OF LIFE] are degrees of an infinite series of failures or abnormalities, or of the attempts of more or less **discouraged** people to solve their life-problems without the use of COOPERATION or SOCIAL INTEREST (p. 299).

> The whole outlook [of the criminal] is conditioned by a socially USELESS GOAL, just as the selection of that GOAL is conditioned by a lack of **courage** (p. 140).

CREATIVE POWER

Adler deferred to the **creative power** of the individual as at the center of human development. From the earliest years, "how the child assimilates impressions" and shapes responses depends upon "the **creative power** of the child" (Adler, 1979, p. 195).

> We must refute the causal significance of situation, milieu, or experiences of the child. Their significance and effectiveness develop only in the intermediary psychological metabolism (p. 178).

> All inherited possibilities and all influences of the body, all environmental influences, including educational application, are perceived, assimilated, digested, and answered by a living and striving being, striving for a successful achievement (p. 178).

> We cannot know in advance what the child will make of [influences and experiences]. . . . Here the child works in the realm of freedom with his own **creative power**. . . . Here there are thousands of possibilities in the realm of freedom and of ERROR (p. 187).

> The **creative** striving of the child takes place in an environment which is individually comprehended and which posits individual difficulties. . . . [A child] depending on a hundred influences and errors, can never be comprehended causally (pp. 184-185).

> Every individual represents both a UNITY of personality and the individual fashioning of that UNITY. The individual is thus both the picture and the artist (p. 177).

> Who can say that the same ENVIRONMENTAL influences are apprehended, worked over, digested, and responded to by any two individuals the same way? To understand this fact we find it necessary to assume the existence of still another force, the **creative power** of the individual (pp. 176-177).

DEGREE OF ACTIVITY

Adler attended to differences in the **degree of activity** incorporated in the STYLE OF LIVING, regarding this **degree of activity** to be an independent variable as an indicator of the individual's LAW OF MOVEMENT. It must be noted that **activity** is a PHENOMENOLOGICAL term, referring to what is observable, and that it is used in deliberate contrast to "energy," often referred to as if held in a "level," in more speculative postulations. That being said, we should also note here that Adler was not scrupulous in maintaining the distinction, as one can see in the first citation below, where he speaks incautiously of the **degree of activity** as if of a quantifiable substance that could be stored and held in "supply" throughout life. (This can be cited as an incidence of Adler's "carelessness" in theoretical writing, as Heinz Ansbacher once called it in a moment of exasperation [H. L. Ansbacher, personal communication, n.d.]).

> The **degree of activity** acquired in childhood becomes a constant supply which endures throughout life (p. 164).

> Although it is probably not possible to express the **degree of activity** in quantitative terms, it is obvious that a child who runs away from his parents, or a boy who starts a fight in the street, must be credited with a higher **degree of activity** than a child who likes to sit at home and read a book (Adler, 1978, p. 60).

> Among the most important structures of . . . [the] STYLE OF LIFE are a definite **degree of activity** and definite degree of SOCIAL INTEREST which gives the direction to that **activity** (p. 164).

> *NEUROSIS is the natural, logical development of an individual who is comparatively **inactive**, filled with a personal, egocentric STRIVING FOR SUPERIORITY, and is therefore retarded in the development of his SOCIAL INTEREST*, as we find regularly among the more passive PAMPERED STYLES OF LIFE (p. 241).

> Comparatively more **active** children [who manifest the pampered STYLE OF LIFE] are much less in danger of becoming NEUROTICS. At a given moment, always dependent upon an EXOGENOUS FACTOR, that is, a difficult situation, they tend to become criminals (p. 241).

DEPRECIATION TENDENCY

The **depreciation tendency** is the practiced MOVEMENT of the discouraged individual to "enhance his self-esteem by disparaging" others (p. 268). **Depreciation** of others may take the form of belittling them, of putting them on pedestals only to attack them when they reveal themselves to be capable of shortcomings or mistakes, or of worrying about them as if they were not competent to manage their own lives. The **depreciation** of others "secures some triumph" for the individual — or "at least allays the fear of defeat" (p. 269).

> It is the **depreciation tendency** which underlies the phenomenon Freud described as RESISTANCE and erroneously understood as the consequence of the repression of SEXUAL impulses (p. 337).

> Every patient will attempt to **depreciate** the physician (p. 337).

> A basic principle for the therapist is never to allow the patient to force upon him a superior role such as that of teacher, father, or savior, without contradicting and enlightening the patient. Such attempts represent the beginning of a MOVEMENT on the part of the patient to pull down, in a manner to which he has been previously accustomed, all persons standing above him, and by thus administering a defeat, to disavow them (p. 339).

> Those who can't be big, belittle. (R. Dreikurs, as cited in Carlson, J., Watts, R. E., & Maniacci, M. P., p. 145).

DETHRONEMENT

Adler employed the word **dethronement** to capture the drama of the first-born child's experience of his situation at the second-born's birth and subsequent incorporation into the FAMILY CONSTELLATION. Varieties of the upheaval can be seen in the experience of later-born children at the births of their younger siblings as well, perhaps especially when a child has enjoyed some time as a favored "baby." One man, the youngest of four children in a farm family until he was five years old, when a fifth child was born, reported a family story about him (not his own EARLY RECOLLECTION), telling that he had been asked what he thought should be done with the newcomer. Without hesitation he replied, "I think we should feed him to the pigs." (Adler was not beyond flattering his own vanity when in regard to this concept of **dethronement** he remarked upon his advance ahead of other theorists — not least Freud, as the second quotation, below, illustrates.) [See PSYCHOLOGICAL BIRTH ORDER POSITION/BIRTH ORDER VANTAGE.]

> Sometimes a child who has lost his power, the small kingdom he ruled, understands better than others the importance of power and authority. When he grows up, he likes to take part in the exercise of authority and exaggerates the importance of rules and laws (pp. 378-379).

> The first-born is in a unique situation; for a while he is an only child and sometime later he is "**dethroned**." This expression chosen by me depicts the change in the situation so exactly that later writers, as Freud, for example, when they do justice to such a case, cannot do without this figurative expression (p. 377).

> When other children lose their position in the same way [as the first born], they will probably not feel it as strongly, since they have already had the experience of COOPERATING with another child. They have never been the sole object of consideration and care (p. 378).

DREAMS /DAYDREAMS /FANTASIES

Dreams, daydreams, and **fantasies** can all be understood as activities of the individual consistent with and expressive of the LIFESTYLE. Adler includes **day** and **night dreams** among the five categories essential for exploring LIFESTYLE (pp. 327-328). While Adler acknowledged that Freud was first in recognizing the value of studying patient **dreams** ("We must honor him for laying the foundation of the science of **dream** interpretation"), he also said, in a kind of second-born son's back-handed comment on a first-born son's priority, that he "learned from [Freud's] mistakes" and rejected Freud's idea that **dream** content has to do with infantile sexual wishes or death wishes (p. 358).

Adler's understanding is that an individual's **dreams, daydreams**, and **fantasies** inhere in the UNITY of the personality, and therefore that "only by considering **dreams** as one of the expressions of the STYLE OF LIFE may an adequate interpretation of them be found" (p. 359). **Dreams** serve a problem-solving function by moving the individual toward solutions, operating as "a bridge that connects the problem which confronts the dreamer [the EXOGENOUS FACTOR] with his GOAL of attainment" (p. 359). Adler, who claimed that he never **dreamed**, thought that people with COMMUNITY FEELING hardly ever dream, since they solve their problems in waking life. (Research affirms Adler's view that the function of **dreaming** is to problem-solve, but disproves his notion about the incidence of **dreaming**, showing that everyone who sleeps **dreams** every night [Cartwright, 1997]). Dreikurs (1973) quotes Adler as saying that **dreams** are "the factory of the EMOTIONS" (p. 221), and it is the EMOTIONS that serve as preparation for action: "The golden rule of INDIVIDUAL PSYCHOLOGY is: 'Everything can be different.' We must modify each **dream** interpretation to fit the individual concerned. . . . The only valid **dream** interpretation is that which can be integrated with an individual's general behavior" (p. 363).

[On Sunday, June 18, 1989 the *London Observer* reported that a "previously unknown manuscript by Sigmund Freud, in which the founder of psychoanalysis describes **dreams** of appearing naked in public and failing crucial examinations, has been discovered in the archives of a European family. It is understood to have been written privately for Alfred Adler, one of Freud's most influential disciples [*sic*]."]

> The **dream** purposefully creates an EMOTIONAL state in the **dreamer** (Shulman, 1973, p. 63).
>
> The meaning of **dreams** can be recognized by an objective and trained interpreter by looking for the PURPOSE which the **dream** situation might have in the actual life situation of the **dreamer**. Without knowledge of the patient's problems and conflicts, no **dream** can be accurately interpreted (Dreikurs, 1973, p. 221).
>
> [A client's] made-up **dreams** are just as good as his genuinely remembered **dreams,** for his imagination and **fantasy** will also be an expression of his STYLE OF LIFE (Adler, 1969, p. 70).
>
> The **fantasies** of children and grownups, sometimes called **daydreams**, are always concerned with the future. The[se] "castles in the air" are . . . built up in FICTIONAL form as models for real activity (Adler, 1957, p. 56).
>
> The INFERIORITY FEELING finally culminates in a never-ceasing, always exaggerated FEELING of being slighted, so that the Cinderella **fantasy** becomes complete with its longing expectation of redemption and triumph. The frequent **fantasies** of children regarding their princely origin and temporary banishment from their "real" home are of this kind (p. 53).

EARLY RECOLLECTIONS

Early recollections are stories of single, specific incidents in childhood which the individual is able to reconstitute in present experience as mental images or as focused sensory memories. They are understood dynamically; that is, the act of recollecting and remembering is a present activity, the historical validity of which is irrelevant to present PURPOSE. They are considered to be projective (Mosak, 1977), therefore, INDIVIDUAL PSYCHOLOGY understands **early recollections** as mirroring presently-held CONVICTIONS, evaluations, attitudes, and biases. Individuals usually retain only a few **early recollections** that come to mind in response to chance stimuli or upon inquiry, in either case without explicit awareness of meaning or purpose. They may be thought of by analogy to the myths of the peoples that validate and sanctify the practices and values of a cultural form (Powers, 1973). As personal myths they are similarly held in memory and periodically REHEARSED for PURPOSES of individual identity and orientation. **Early recollections** are examined for their implications as they come to be reported in the course of therapy, either at the initiative of client or counselor. For example, in response to the client's report of a troublesome FEELING, the counselor may ask, "Can you remember the first time in your life you felt this way?" In the **recollection** that comes in response they may recover the CONTEXT of the original shock reaction, reappearing in the current FEELING as a caution or expectation directed toward an apparent similarity in the client's current situation and challenges. Further, the systematic gathering and interpretation of a set of **early recollections** is a component of LIFESTYLE ASSESSMENT. [See ERRORS/BASIC MISTAKES/INTERFERING IDEAS.]

> Among all psychological expressions, some of the most revealing are the individual's memories. His memories are the reminders he carries about with him of his own limits and of the meaning of circumstances (p. 351).

> There are no "chance memories": out of the incalculable number of impressions which meet an individual, he chooses to remember only those which he feels, however darkly, to have a bearing on his situation (p. 351).

> The first memory will show . . . [the individual's] fundamental view of life, his first satisfactory crystallization of his attitude (p. 351).

> If we have found the real LAW OF MOVEMENT in an individual's **recollections**, we will find the same law confirmed in all his other forms of expression (p. 354).

> Memory, like attention, is selective, in keeping with the economy of the mind and the PURPOSES of the individual. Actively to remember everything, even if it were possible, would so clutter and fill attention that it is difficult to imagine how we could endure it. The theoretical problem, therefore, is to account not for the fact that we forget so much (which is the burden of theories of *repression*), but rather for the fact that we remember what we do (Powers & Griffith, 1987, p. 185).

> INDIVIDUAL PSYCHOLOGY is a theory of *expression*. It assumes that we retain these particular memories in order to maintain an orientation through time, to REHEARSE our UNDERSTANDING of the fundamental issues of life, and to provide ourselves with reminders of the reliability of our CONVICTIONS (Powers & Griffith, 1987, p. 185).

See Clark, A. J. (2002); Maniacci, M. P., Shulman, B., Griffith, J., Powers, R. L., Sutherland, J., Dushman, R., Schneider, M. F., (1998).

EDUCATION/GUIDANCE

Because of his UNDERSTANDING that the prototype of the LIFESTYLE is formed in the earliest years of life, Adler was particularly devoted to the successful development of children. Dreikurs followed Adler's lead in directing his major energies to guiding PARENTS and teachers in **educating** and TRAINING children, and, like Adler, in emphasizing the EQUALITY of dignity of adults and children.

Adler emphasized that the schoolroom is a community and that class meetings are a way to bring students together to help each other and solve classroom problems. Dreikurs, Grunwald, and Pepper (1971), in a section titled "Effective Democratic Methods," present a program for teacher-pupil and pupil-pupil interaction for creating a classroom community (pp. 54-185). [See PARENTING; MISTAKEN GOALS OF THE DISCOURAGED CHILD.]

> The school is placed between the family and life in society. It has the opportunity of correcting the MISTAKEN STYLES OF LIFE formed under family upbringing, and the responsibility of preparing the child's ADJUSTMENT to social life so that he will play his individual role harmoniously in the orchestral pattern of society (p. 399).

> An **educator's** most important task, one might almost say his holy duty, is to see to it that no child is DISCOURAGED at school and that a child who enters school already DISCOURAGED regains his self-confidence through his school and his teacher (pp. 399-400).

> The **educational** plan must aim particularly at bringing the child to self-reliance of judgment, at making him more independent of the opinion of others, and at setting up substitute goals [to replace MISTAKEN GOALS] (p. 55).

> **Educational** influences are likely to be accepted only when they seem to hold a promise of success for the individual's STYLE OF LIFE (p. 212).

See Adler, A. (1930); Dreikurs, R. (1974); for information on *Corsini 4R Schools* based on Adlerian Psychology, see Painter, G., & Corsini, R. J. (1990); Walton, F. X., & Powers, R. L. (1974).

EMBEDDEDNESS/SOCIAL EMBEDDEDNESS

In regarding the human being as an inherently social being, Adler argued that the individual cannot be considered or understood apart from the social and historical CONTEXT in which he or she plays a part, whether positively as a contributor or negatively as a locus of disturbance. Adler therefore considered individual problems as, by implication, social problems that require the COOPERATION of others for their solution. Any HESITATION of a child to address these problems directly reveals a failure of the child's caretakers to provide trustworthy alliances, sufficient ENCOURAGEMENT, and realistic EDUCATION concerning the requirements of life. In an adult, HESITATION reflects shortcomings in the person's TRAINING and preparation for COOPERATIVE and productive participation in the life of the community. The individual's psychological difficulties must therefore be examined with a consideration of the social CONTEXT in which they arise. (Adler's social orientation reflects his fundamental difference from Freud, who imagined human being on the model of a spoiled child, for whom the requirements of social living are antagonistic to personal gratification.)

> INDIVIDUAL PSYCHOLOGY accepts the viewpoint of the complete UNITY and self-consistency of the individual whom it regards and examines as **socially embedded**. We refuse to recognize and examine an isolated human being (p. 126).

> The style or the pattern of a child's life cannot be understood without reference to the persons who look after him and who make up for his INFERIORITY. The child has interlocking relations with the mother and family which could never be understood if we confined our analysis to the periphery of the child's physical being in space. The individuality of the child cuts across his physical individuality, it involves a whole CONTEXT of social relations (p. 127).

> When we consider that not even the conditions of human relations can be fully comprehended because they are too numerous and further that these demands are subject to change, then it becomes clear that we are scarcely in a position to gain complete insight into the darknesses of a given psychological life (p. 128).

> If the conditions of life are determined in the first instance by cosmic influences, they are in the second instance determined socially. They are determined by the fact that men live together and by the rules and regularities which spontaneously arise in consequence of this. The demands of society have regulated human relations which had already existed from the beginning as self-understood, as an absolute truth. For before the individual life of man there was the community. In the history of human culture, there is not a single form of life which was not conducted as social. Never has man appeared otherwise than in society (p. 128).

EMOTIONS (FEELINGS)

The **emotions** were, for Adler, to be considered and understood apart from speculations concerning their origins in the operations of the nervous or endocrine systems. He was respectful of the variety of habitual **emotional** patterns predominant in different individuals, and he did not rule out the likelihood of their being discovered to be HEREDITARY in origin. Allowing that their primary forms could be identified in the responses to certain shocks experienced by infant and child, and in a mental tension then communicated and felt throughout the body by means of the autonomic system, Adler found the meaning of such events in whether they were clung to and rehearsed, instead of being allowed to pass from awareness after the moment of their occurrence. Adler regarded this clinging and REHEARSING to be the work of the individual, molding the expression of **feelings** into forms consistent with his or her STYLE OF LIVING, in line with a personal GOAL. He differentiated among these expressions as either socially disjunctive (G., *trennende Affekte*) as in anger, sadness, misuse of emotion, disgust, and fear and anxiety; or conjunctive (G., *verbindende Affekte*) as in joy, sympathy, and modesty (an affect which he says can be both conjunctive and disjunctive). (Adler, 1957, pp. 209-218). Also see Beecher, M. & Beecher, W., 1972, on jealousy. [Note that INFERIORITY FEELING and COMMUNITY FEELING are not included as **emotions**, but carry a different meaning, namely a *sense* of things as they are in reality, independent of **emotion** or opinion.]

Readers of Adler will not be unimpressed by his foreshadowings of the work of later distinguished contributors to human UNDERSTANDING. Hans Selye (1907-1982) in his identification of the *general adaptation syndrome* (1956/1978) uses the term *stress* in much the same way *tension* is used by Adler. Karen Horney (1885-1952), who departed from Freud's psychoanalytic assumptions on much the same grounds as Adler had many years before, is often credited with having introduced the terms "conjunctive" and "disjunctive" into psychological discourse regarding the **emotions**, although the priority is almost certainly Adler's, who used both terms in *Understanding Human Nature* (1927/1957). (It is possible that Horney failed to acknowledge Adler's contribution of these terms because of being not yet sufficiently independent of psychoanalytic domination to defy Freud's well-known edict against citing Adler.)

> The **feelings** of an individual bear the impress of the meaning he gives to life and of the GOAL he has set for his STRIVINGS. To a great extent they rule his body and do not depend on it (p. 226).

> **Feelings** always agree with the GOAL of SUPERIORITY, and should not be regarded as arguments (Adler, 1969, p. 117).

> Joy does not brook isolation (Adler, 1957, p. 216).

> We cannot have anger without an enemy . . . its PURPOSE is a victory over this enemy (Adler, 1957, p. 209).

> **Emotions** . . . have a definite GOAL and direction (Adler, 1957, p. 209).

> [Affects] occur whenever they are appropriate to the given STYLE OF LIFE and the predetermined behavior pattern of the individual. Their PURPOSE is to modify the situation of the individual in whom they occur, to his benefit (Adler, 1957, p. 209).

> INDIVIDUAL PSYCHOLOGY has an axiom that behavior is organized toward a final GOAL and that **emotions** are the catalysts of action (Shulman, 1973, p. 63).

EQUALITY/INEQUALITY

To Dreikurs, **equality** was perhaps the most important emphasis in Adler's thought, and Dreikurs named his last book, *Social Equality: The Challenge of Today* (1971). Adler certainly examined all interpersonal conflicts as reflecting some failure to UNDERSTAND and answer the universal demand for mutual respect between nations, races, sexes, employers-employees, and adults-children. Adler was chary about use of the term **equality** in discussion of human relationships, as the word refers to a mathematical concept, and can carry a connotation of sameness. His emphasis was on the UNIQUENESS of the INDIVIDUAL VARIANT, and he avoided suggestions that we are all the same or can be expected to achieve in the same way as others. He was clear about acknowledging an **equality** of value, especially in intimate relationships, and his recurring references to the commandment, "Thou shalt love thy neighbor as thyself," show that he saw the individual as obliged to grant the same dignity to others which he seeks for himself.

Dr. Kenneth B. Clark (1915-2005), the first African-American president of the American Psychological Association, said that by his study and use of Adler's work, he was able to shape his powerfully influential notes for the argument before the Supreme Court against the "separate but **equal**" doctrine originating in the case of "Plessy v. Ferguson" (1896). Clark's brief argued that "separate" was inherently "**unequal**" in public schools, where it served to undermine the purposes of education by fostering FEELINGS OF INFERIORITY instead of stimulating efforts to OVERCOME such feelings in STRIVING toward positive achievements. This led to the historic 1954 decision, "Brown v. Board of Education of Topeka Kansas" that overturned "Plessy" and so put an end to legal support for racially segregated schools in the United States. Dr. Clark reported that Thurgood Marshall, the lead attorney in the case (later to serve as the first African-American Justice on the Court) told him: "[Chief] Justice [Earl] Warren specifically mentioned the psychological testimony as the key" to winning the case. In an address to the (then) American Society of Adlerian Psychology's 15th Annual Meeting in New York City, Dr. Clark stated:

> My introduction to the theories of Alfred Adler was a turning point in my personal and intellectual life. Adlerian ideas have dominated my professional writings and my actions as a person and as a psychologist from my undergraduate days. . . . To the extent I have been able to make any contribution to the theoretical and moral assumptions upon which the struggle for racial justice in America has been based, it has been primarily through the appropriate modification and use of the Adlerian perspective and conceptual framework. To the extent that Adlerian thinking influenced my own thinking and research, and . . . that my thoughts and writings have influenced in any way the civil rights movement, determines, at least in part, the extent to which ideas of Alfred Adler have contributed to the accelerated quest for racial justice in America (Clark, 1967, pp. 181-190).

> We are approaching a time where everyone will take his place as an **equal**, self-reliantly and freely, no longer in the service of a person, but in the service of a common idea, the idea of physical and mental progress (p. 55).

> It has been imputed to us that we assume and strive for the sameness of men. This is a myth. Quite on the contrary, we attempt to examine the nuances, the UNIQUENESS of the GOAL, the UNIQUENESS of the opinion of a man of himself and the TASKS OF LIFE. The task of INDIVIDUAL PSYCHOLOGY is to comprehend the INDIVIDUAL VARIANT (p. 180).

> INDIVIDUAL PSYCHOLOGY . . . postulates the **equality** of all human life — not to be interpreted as **equality** of achievement (Adler, 1979, p. 284).

> If the [intimate] partners are really interested in each other, there will never be the difficulty of SEXUAL attraction coming to an end. This stop implies always a lack of interest; it tells us that the individual no longer feels **equal**, friendly, and COOPERATIVE toward the partner (p. 433).

ERRORS/BASIC MISTAKES/INTERFERING IDEAS

These three terms refer to those **mistaken** convictions at the base of the individual's STYLE OF LIVING that have led to a faulty ADAPTATION and some lack of success in meeting one or more of the challenges of life. Although these terms may be used interchangeably, each has its own resonance. The **errors** (Adler), **basic mistakes** (Dreikurs), or **interfering ideas** (Powers) are isolated during the process of LIFE-STYLE ASSESSMENT/ LIFE-STYLE DIAGNOSIS.

In INDIVIDUAL PSYCHOLOGY treatment . . . we are always able to draw attention to **errors** only and never to innate defects (p. 342).

Each . . . [individual] organizes himself according to his personal view of things, and some views are more sound, some less sound. We must always reckon with these individual **mistakes** and failures in the development of the human being. Especially must we reckon with the misinterpretations made in early childhood, for these dominate the subsequent course of our existence (p. 183).

The EARLY RECOLLECTIONS show the conclusions . . . [a person] drew from the situation as he perceived it. . . . These conclusions permit the formulation of the **Basic Mistakes** which . . . [were] made in his childhood and maintained throughout life (Dreikurs, 1973, p. 101).

Some . . . have used the terms "**basic mistakes**," "fundamental **errors**," or "erroneous convictions" for what we call **Interfering Ideas**. We prefer our name because it presents the client with an awareness of the **interfering** quality of the trouble these **ideas** introduce, as an added cost in the business of life. Because it does not hint at anything more dire or durable or "**basic**" to deal with than ideas, it seems to us to be a more encouraging term. Whatever the nomenclature, these . . . [LIFE-STYLE] summaries are based on an UNDERSTANDING of the same data, namely, the core sample of the LIFE-STYLE found in the client's EARLY RECOLLECTIONS (Powers & Griffith, 1987, p. 265).

EVOLUTION/SOCIAL EVOLUTION

Adler was a daring theorist, defiant of mechanistic and reductionist assumptions regarding matter and spirit as these things were understood in the Cartesian schema. Mind and body were, to him, combined in the UNITY of the organism, and living organisms were developments, not out of "dead matter" (as it was called), but of matter inherently capable of life. He was, therefore, a radical **evolutionist** whose term SOCIAL EMBEDDEDNESS emphasized the co-inherence of each individual's existence in the existence of the human community. He considered this co-inherence to include the continuity between human life and all life, and, finally, he rejected any notions of discontinuity between life and the cosmos in which it has arisen. To Adler the development of each person takes part in the development of the human community, and the development of the community takes part in the continuing **evolution** of the universe toward the GOAL of perfection.

> INDIVIDUAL PSYCHOLOGY stands firmly on the ground of **evolution** and, in the light of it, regards all human STRIVING for perfection. Bodily and psychologically, the urge to life is tied unalterably to this STRIVING (p. 106).

> The STRIVING for perfection is innate as something which belongs to life, a STRIVING, an urge, a developing, a something without which one could not even conceive of life (Adler, 1979, p. 31).

> How life came on this earth is an uncertain matter; possibly we shall never reach a final answer. We could assume that there is life even in inanimate matter, as for example the ingenious attempt of Smuts [see References] has done (Adler, 1979, p. 32).

> The psychological archetype (*Urform*) of the line of human MOVEMENT is the STRIVING for perfection (p. 114).

EXISTENTIALISM

Existential questions are those addressing the meaning of existence and death, and the problem of personal awareness of one's place in the universe. **Existentialism** as a movement in philosophy includes those who take the position that the universe is indifferent, even hostile, to the human being, who is seen as isolated and alone and necessarily limited, and who, without a GOD, makes choices, under only the authority of individual responsibility that one would want all human beings to make if similarly challenged. In this view, it is ethical behavior that leads to self-transcendence.

INDIVIDUAL PSYCHOLOGY is an **existential** psychology in that it concerns itself with personal meaning, personal responsibility, and ethical choices. It separates itself from **Existentialism** in that INDIVIDUAL PSYCHOLOGY sees human being as SOCIALLY EMBEDDED, sees the development of COMMUNITY FEELING as essential to life, and identifies individual STRIVING toward perfection as present on both the USEFUL and USELESS SIDE. In pursuing GOALS of personal SUPERIORITY on the USELESS SIDE, the STRIVING is erroneous, misunderstanding the reality of its EMBEDDEDNESS, and therefore in need of guidance and EDUCATION toward GOALS on the USEFUL SIDE, CONCRETIZED in images of CONTRIBUTION and self-transcendence, whether in the ideal community (as envisioned *sub specie aeternitatis*), or in GOD.

> None of us knows which is the only correct way toward perfection. Mankind has variously made the attempt to imagine this final GOAL of human development. The best conception gained so far of this ideal elevation of mankind is the concept of GOD (Jahn and Adler). There is no question but that the concept of GOD actually includes this MOVEMENT toward perfection in the form of a GOAL, and that as a CONCRETE GOAL of perfection it corresponds best to man's dark longing to reach perfection (Adler, 1979, p. 33).

> There are, of course, countless attempts among men to imagine this GOAL of perfection differently. . . . When, for example, someone attempts to CONCRETIZE this GOAL by wanting to dominate over others, such a GOAL of perfection appears to us incapable to steer the individual and the group. The reason is that not every one could make this GOAL of perfection his task, because he would be forced to come into conflict with the coercion of EVOLUTION, to violate reality, and to defend himself full of anxiety against the truth and its confessors (Adler, 1979, p. 33).

> To be a human being means to have INFERIORITY FEELINGS. One recognizes one's own power-lessness in the face of nature. One sees death as the irrefutable consequence of existence (G., *Man sieht den Todt als unabweisliche Konsequenz des Daseins*). But in the mentally healthy person this INFERIORITY FEELING acts as a motive for productivity, as a motive for attempting to OVERCOME obstacles, to maintain oneself in life (Adler, 1979, p. 54).

EXOGENOUS FACTOR

Exogenous factor means something arising outside of, and independent of one's own agency. It signifies a challenge, a shift, or an interruption in the course of life demanding a response which, on the basis of his or her prior TRAINING AND SELF-TRAINING, the individual feels unprepared to meet with COOPERATIVE and COURAGEOUS action. Such a challenge to the practiced adaptation of the LIFESTYLE may be a particular event in the individual's life, or may be one of the universally experienced alterations of status, such as occur in the transition between childhood and ADOLESCENCE, that is, at the point at which the first adult choices and expectations may be assumed to impose their imperatives. In therapy, the **exogenous factor**, if not in the client's awareness, may be uncovered with the question (asked with reference to the reported onset of symptoms): "What else was going on in your life at the time?" Investigating and understanding "the nature of the **exogenous factor**" (p. 328) that prompts generation of the symptom, is one of the "most trustworthy approaches to the exploration of personality" (p. 327). [See ADLERIAN PSYCHOTHERAPY.]

> The onset of the symptoms takes place when a person is confronted by a certain problem. . . . [Our studies] have shown that people are always confronted with problems which require a social preparation for their solution. . . . Such preparation must be acquired in earliest childhood (p. 295).

> The **exogenous factor**, the proximity of a task that demands COOPERATION and fellowship, is always the exciting factor of the symptoms, the behavior problem (pp. 297-298).

FACTOPHILIA

Factophilia is a neologism often used by Dreikurs to characterize a "disease" (as he called it) that afflicts counselors and therapists who persist in collecting increasing amounts of data, AS IF the data — if only one has enough of it — will, in itself, reveal the truth about a client's difficulty.

Dreikurs compared followers of this method to someone who is collecting ceramic tiles, hoping that when there is a large enough number of them a mosaic will appear. The pattern is what is wanted, and that begins to emerge from GUESSING, after one has a few, or even only two facts. (R. Dreikurs, personal communication, n. d.) [See TWO POINTS ON A LINE.]

According to H.L. Ansbacher (personal communication, July 3, 1984), "Regarding 'factophilia' Dreikurs did not coin the term. It was coined by Henry Winthrop, a friend of [Abraham] Maslow, in a very good paper, 'Scientism in Psychology' (*Journal of Individual Psychology,* 1959, 15, 112-120). Dreikurs originally credited Winthrop."

FAMILY ATMOSPHERE/FAMILY VALUES

These terms were introduced by Dreikurs (1964). They have been relied upon by his students, and the students of his students, in examining and interpreting family dynamics in LIFE-STYLE ASSESSMENT and family counseling. Powers and Griffith (1987) have expanded upon Dreikurs's original observations in an effort to make explicit what we believe he implied by the way he used them.

Powers and Griffith portray the **family atmosphere** as set by the emotional tone of the relationship between the parents and/or other adults constituting the household of the family of origin. We describe it in a figure of speech as the climate of the household as the person remembers perceiving and experiencing it in childhood. As a term, **family atmosphere** employs meteorological imagery to convey a sense of the ambience in which **values** are planted and cultivated. For example, the **atmosphere** may be referred to as sunny, warm, calm, or salubrious; tense, stormy, threatening, or cold. It may also be described as transactional, in ways varying from encouraging, cooperative, and caring to denigrating or hostile. Evaluations of **family atmosphere** are the background for judgments made about life in early childhood when the individual's BASIC CONVICTIONS about self, others, and the world were being formed; therefore, these valuations have significance in illuminating the CONTEXT of his or her BIASED APPERCEPTIONS and continuing expectations about what life both provides and requires. [See MOST MEMORABLE OBSERVATION.]

Family values are those **values** *shared* by mother and father; that is, **values** which the children perceive to be important to both parents. Such **values** operate as *imperatives*: Each child will feel obliged to take up a position in regard to them. Any one of the children may, for example, support them, subvert them, ignore them, or defy them by taking a contrary position. Those **values** *not* shared by the parents, but held only by one or the other, do not have the same significance: Children are likely to experience these unshared **values** as features of the GENDER GUIDING LINES.

> There are . . . [certain] factors in the child's outer environment which affect the development of his personality. The first is the *family atmosphere*. In his relationship with his parents the child experiences society at large. The parents establish a definite **family atmosphere**; through them the child experiences the economic, racial, religious, and social influences in his environment. He absorbs the **family values**, mores, and conventions, and tries to fit within the pattern, or the standards, set by the PARENTS. . . . If PARENTS look down upon people who are different, children may . . . seek superiority in racial and social relationships. . . . Children are also quick to observe how the PARENTS treat each other (Dreikurs, 1964, pp.18-19).

> The child evaluates the **family atmosphere**, set by the attitudinal and operational relationship between the PARENTS, and between the PARENTS and the world (including the children), and concludes, "This is what I have to expect and prepare for in my dealings with others" (Powers & Griffith, 1987, p. 23).

> The child considers the **values** that are shared by the PARENTS, and concludes, "These are the issues of central importance, on which I must be prepared to take a stand" (Powers & Griffith, 1987, p. 23).

FAMILY CONSTELLATION

Family constellation is the term coined by Adler and elaborated by Dreikurs to represent the operation of the **family** system, including PARENTS, siblings, and others in the family of origin, together with any others living with them as members of the person's childhood household. It pictures the family by analogy to a **constellation** in astronomy, a group of bodies in motion, each of which has its place in relation to the places of the others. In clarifying the origins of a LIFESTYLE, this image is intended to help clients consider how they MADE, TOOK, or FOUND, PLACES for themselves from the beginning, and so to understand their REHEARSALS of unique patterns of MOVEMENT for FINDING and holding PLACES in circles of the wider social world. [See PSYCHOLOGICAL BIRTH ORDER POSITION/BIRTH ORDER VANTAGE.]

> A clear formulation of a person's LIFE STYLE can be obtained through investigation of his **family constellation**, which is a sociogram of the group at home during his formative years. This investigation reveals his field of early experiences, the circumstances under which he developed his personal perspectives and biases, his concepts and convictions about himself and others, his fundamental attitudes, and his own approaches to life, which are the basis for his character, his personality (Dreikurs, 1973, p. 87).

> The PSYCHOCLARITY PROCESS rests upon a thorough appreciation of the CONTEXT in which the inevitable ERRORS made by a child can be understood as having made a certain kind of sense. . . . The LIFE-STYLE ASSESSMENT procedure . . . calls for a thorough inquiry into the particularities of the situation in which this one person learned to REHEARSE and to make do with a particular pattern of ERRORS (Powers & Griffith, 1987, pp. 20-21).

> We systematically record a thorough description of the members of the person's FAMILY of origin, their relationships, and their circumstances. This gives us a sense of the social dynamics and organization (the "**family constellation**") in which the person encountered the TASKS OF LIFE (Powers & Griffith, 1987, p. 67).

> [A boy] . . . was for five years the only child of PARENTS who had seen better days. . . . His great deterioration dates from the time his sister was born and began to play a part in the **family constellation** (Adler, 1930, pp. 26-27).

FAMILY COUNCIL/FAMILY MEETING

These terms are used interchangeably. The idea of the **family council** was developed by Dreikurs (1974) as a vehicle for promoting democratic leadership, family harmony, individual responsibility, and mutually respectful engagement in problem-solving. Briefly, families (including all members of a household who choose to attend) meet at an agreed-upon fixed time and place each week to (a) plan family activities; (b) discuss and decide upon the assignment of household tasks; (c) discuss difficulties, suggest solutions to problems, and agree on LOGICAL CONSEQUENCES. All family members may put items on the agenda for the meeting. Responsibilities for chairing the **family meeting,** and for recording minutes of decisions reached, rotate among members. Decisions are unanimous. If no decision is reached on a matter, the family thereby signifies that it is willing to leave that situation as it is for the present; the matter may be put on the agenda for further discussion at the following week's meeting. Decisions may remain in effect for as little as one week only, or until whatever time they are reviewed, evaluated for their effectiveness, and reworked as needed. The purpose of the **family meeting** is not the construction of a perfect or permanent order; rather it is a means for fostering the solidarity of the family in the management of its life, as it is being lived, week by week.

See Dreikurs, R., Gould, S., & Corsini, R. J. (1974); McKay, G. D. & Maybell, S. A. (2004).

FELT MINUS AND FELT (FICTIONAL) PLUS

Felt minus and **felt plus** are Adler's shorthand terms for the INFERIORITY FEELING and its COMPENSATIONS. The **felt minus** describes the universally-experienced INFERIORITY FEELINGS of incompleteness, of being below, of being in a position of "less than" the others, or less than what life requires or allows.

Adler's **felt plus** is more accurately understood as a *fictional* **plus,** that is, a subjectively-constructed (hence fictional) image of maturity, mastery, completion, fulfillment, or perfection which the individual STRIVES to attain in his or her struggle to MOVE away from the **felt minus** situation toward the **fictional plus** PERSONALITY IDEAL.

> The impetus from **minus** to **plus** never ends. The urge from below to above never ceases (p. 103).

> The whole of human life proceeds along this great line of action — from below to above, from **minus** to **plus**, from defeat to victory (p. 255).

FEMINISM

In the early days of Adler's period (1870 – 1937), in the cultural world of Imperial Austria, it was a given that girls and women were INFERIOR to boys and men. "This myth of the INFERIORITY of everything female," Adler stated, results in a "dichotomy of concepts: Masculine is simply identified with valuable, strong, and victorious, and feminine with obedient, servile, and subordinated" (Adler, 1978, p. 8).

Most women of that day accepted their INFERIORITY as a verity, though some resisted by adopting roles then associated with men. Others, unable in such an atmosphere even to UNDERSTAND or state their resistance openly, fought UNCONSCIOUSLY to subvert the dominant order by means of ORGAN DIALECT (as in vaginismus or hysteria). Still others, called **feminists**, dared voice their demands for EQUALITY in both the private and public spheres. Adler, influenced by Marxist ideals of EQUALITY and justice, was a **feminist**. He joined the Socialist party (whose platform in 1885 was the first in history to embrace the EQUALITY of women). He later married Raissa Epstein (a Muscovite who had come to Vienna to study), also a **feminist** and socialist. Adler was politically active until he formed the Comparative INDIVIDUAL PSYCHOLOGY Society, from which time he devoted himself to the development of his psychology, never losing sight of the need for social change.

Throughout the development of Adlerian theory and practice, Adler's **feminism** never wavered. In addition to supporting demands for economic, social, and political EQUALITY, he addressed such issues as reforming bias in language, equal pay for equal work, obstacles for women arising from their employment, and women's role in family planning.

> The arch evil of our culture [is] the excessive pre-eminence of manliness (p. 55).

> The number of men who show no accomplishments but a high degree of incompetence is so great that one could defend with an equal mass of evidence a myth of the INFERIORITY of men — of course, equally unjustly (Adler, 1978, p. 8).

> Art, like science, so far has been almost exclusively the work of men and reflects primarily man's [opinions taken as] knowledge of the female soul. . . . The masculine preponderance among these opinions is certainly an evil (Adler, 1978, pp. 83-84).

> [The] low esteem [in which women are held and in which they hold themselves] is also expressed in far lower pay for women than for men, even when the work is equal in value to men's work (Adler, 1978, p. 7).

> The knowledge of being an unwanted child poisons the life of many individuals [and] plants the root for serious psychological disturbance. . . . Alone in the interest in these children . . . I am in favor of telling every woman very plainly: "You need not have children if you don't want to. . . . [All arguments take a secondary role] compared to this argument: Only a woman who wants the child can be a good mother to him or her (Adler, 1978, p. 30).

> The question of deciding the number of children had best be left entirely to the woman (p. 434).

FICTIONAL GOAL /GUIDING FICTION /FICTIONAL FINALISM

Adler adapted the concept of FICTIONS from the "AS IF" philosophy of Hans Vaihinger (1911/1925). [See "AS IF"/FICTIONS.]

Fictional goal, guiding fiction, and **fictional finalism** are related terms referring to the same feature of psychological COMPENSATION, namely, the individual's UNCONSCIOUS, subjectively conceived, ever-present **goal** of success, the SELF-IDEAL. In the first few years of life, the child creates a **fictional goal** of success that contrasts to and assuages the child's intolerable FEELINGS OF INFERIORITY, evident in the phrase, "Some day when I grow up. . . ." As the person develops, the **goal** continues to operate as a **guiding fiction** in any present situation. It gives direction to the person's MOVEMENT, while shifting to new forms of CONCRETIZATION in the ambitions of adult life: "Only when I am _____ (good, rich, smart, important, in control, etc.), will I be _____ (admired, accepted, secure, significant, etc.)." H. L. and R. R. Ansbacher state that the **fictional final goal** was, for Adler, "the principle of internal, subjective *causation* of psychological events" [italics added] (p. 90). [See GOAL(S); SELF-IDEAL (*PERSÖNLICHKEITSIDEAL*); CONCRETIZATION OF THE GOAL; HIDDEN MEANING/HIDDEN REASON.]

> [From the] standpoint of a low self-evaluation . . . the child's psyche spins threads of thought to the **goals** of his longing (pp. 98-99).

> The **guiding fiction** is originally the means or device by which the child seeks to free himself from his INFERIORITY FEELING (p. 98).

> In each mind there is a conception of a [**fictional**] **goal** or [SELF] IDEAL to get beyond the present state and to overcome the present deficiencies and difficulties. . . . By means of this CONCRETE **goal**, the individual can think and feel himself superior to the difficulties of the present because he has in mind his success of the future (pp. 99-100).

> [The **fictional goal**] can well be understood as a TELEOLOGICAL device of the soul which seeks orientation (p. 93).

> The stronger the feeling of insecurity, the more accentuated the **fiction** becomes through increasing abstraction from reality, and the more it approaches dogma (p. 247).

> [The] **goal** enables us to understand the HIDDEN MEANING behind the various separate acts and to see them as parts of a whole (pp. 92-93).

> The **goal** of the mental life of man becomes its governing principle, its *causa finalis* (p. 94).

FIELD THEORY

This term refers to a psychological theory largely associated with Kurt Lewin, the tenets of which have become foundational to most contemporary psychologies. According to Harre and Lamb (1983), **field theory** assumes that "psychological events must be explained in psychological terms"; that "the proper focus of investigation" is "central processes of the life space (distal perception, cognition, motivation, goal-directed behavior)," not "peripheral processes" such as "sensory input and muscular action"; that the individual "must be studied in inter-relations" to the group he or she belongs to; that "psychological events" must also be studied in inter-relation to other psychological events; and that "social-psychological phenomena can be studied experimentally" (p. 237).

INDIVIDUAL PSYCHOLOGY'S premises and treatments are compatible with **field theory**. H. L. Ansbacher and R. R. Ansbacher (in editorial comments in Adler, 1964) state, "We believe that the understanding of Adler is greatly facilitated if he is regarded as the original **field theorist** in the area of modern dynamic psychology" (p. 13).

GENDER GUIDING LINES AND ROLE MODELS

In LIFESTYLE assessment Dreikurs used Adler's concept of **guiding lines** to delineate a person's ideas about masculine and feminine and what it means to be a man or a woman. To uncover **masculine** and **feminine guiding lines** he considered the way father and mother were remembered from the client's childhood years.

Powers and Griffith (1987) further developed the therapeutic application of the concept of **gender guiding lines**, first, by proposing that a person's childhood images of mother and father form the *norms* for what it means to be a man or a woman, against which all men and women are evaluated; second, that the same-sex **gender guiding line** feels like a *destiny* to the person, AS IF the small child believed, "When I grow up, I'm going to be like that *unless* I do something about it." Further, these expectations form part of a person's PRIVATE SENSE, and so are not likely to be in full CONSCIOUS awareness. **Role models** differ from **gender guiding lines** in that they are chosen or rejected by the child in CONSCIOUS awareness. When a person's same-sex **gender guiding line** and **role models** are *consonant*, one can expect that the individual is clear about gender identity and feels untroubled in his or her gender adaptation. The converse is also predictable: when the **gender guiding line** and **role models** are *dissonant*, one often finds a sense of unease or distress connected with the person's way of addressing the task of love and sexual functioning (Powers & Griffith, 1987, pp. 132-149). [See THE BIG NUMBERS.]

See Powers, R. L., Griffith, J., & Maybell, S. A. (1993).

GOAL(S)

All of life is PURPOSIVE. Human beings, like other living things, move toward their own completeness. For the human being, whether or not in CONSCIOUS awareness, MOVEMENT is oriented forward, toward **goals.** Two **goals** operate constantly: The overarching FICTIONAL GOAL of the personality (SELF-IDEAL), and the immediate **goal**, consistent with the FICTIONAL GOAL, of one's activity in response to life's requirements. To UNDERSTAND a human being is to comprehend his or her **goals**. [See GUIDING FICTION/ FICTIONAL GOAL/FICTIONAL FINALISM; CONCRETIZATION OF THE GOAL; SELF-IDEAL; TELEOLOGY/PURPOSE.]

> *We cannot think, FEEL, will or act without the perception of some **goal**. . . .* All psychic activities are given direction by means of a previously determined **goal**. . . . *Every psychic phenomenon . . . can only be grasped as preparation for some **goal*** (Adler, 1959, pp. 3-4).

> In the case of a psychotherapeutic cure . . . [we examine] first the SUPERIORITY-**goal** (Adler, 1959, p. 13).

> If we know the **goal** of a person, we can undertake to explain and to UNDERSTAND what the psychological phenomena want to tell us, why they were CREATED, what a person has made of his innate material, why he has made it just so and not differently, how his character traits, his FEELINGS and EMOTIONS, his logic, his morals, and his aesthetics must be considered in order that he may arrive at his **goal** (p. 196).

GOD/RELIGION/SPIRITUALITY

Adler worked as a physician and aspired to think and write as a scientist. His understanding of the range of scientific thought was, however, inclusive of a respectful consideration of the PHENOMENA of religious belief, language, and practice. Adler did not write in the tone of one who saw through or condescended toward symbolic forms or devout practices. His science was not meant to dispel "illusions" but to regard religious FICTIONS as necessary devices for an appreciation of realities otherwise inaccessible to strictly scientific inquiry. These FICTIONS remain illustrative as CONCRETIZATIONS OF THE GOAL of human MOVEMENT, which is included in the universal STRIVING of all things toward perfection. One who is not sympathetic to the metaphysic of emergent EVOLUTION in which Adler (1979) situated the study of both physical and psychological PHENOMENA will doubtless find his writings to be elusive, perhaps even exasperating. There will be little argument when he says, "Mankind has variously made the attempt to imagine this final GOAL of human development," or when he goes on to say, "Of course it seems to me that each person imagines his **God** differently." However, those who want an argument can find one when, in the same paragraph he also says, "The best conception gained so far of this ideal elevation of mankind is the concept of **God** (Jahn and Adler)" conceding that "There are conceptions of **God** which from the outset are not equal to the principle of perfection," and then concludes, "But of the purest formulation of **God** we can say: Here the CONCRETE formulation of the GOAL of perfection has been accomplished" (p. 33).

He anticipated argument and complaint, and a little later in the same paper, says "Of course one will ask, how do I know this?" answering, "Certainly not from immediate experience. . . . Those who find a piece of metaphysics in INDIVIDUAL PSYCHOLOGY are right. Some praise this, others criticize it" (Adler, 1979, p. 35).

We do not criticize it. His suggestive and poetic evocation of the MOVEMENT of human STRIVING, and of the place of **religious** thought and practice in that STRIVING, is to us a sign of his intellectual daring.

> The idea of **God** and its immense significance for mankind can be understood and appreciated from the viewpoint of INDIVIDUAL PSYCHOLOGY as CONCRETIZATION and interpretation of the human recognition of greatness and perfection, and as commitment of the individual as well as society to a GOAL which rests in man's future and which in the present heightens the driving force by enhancing the FEELINGS and EMOTIONS (Adler, 1979, p. 276).

> The ideal, ultimate union can hardly be attained, whether one forbids the making of an image or attempts to bring about identity with an image. No wonder that in the millionfold diversity of CONCRETIZATION the scale ranges all the way from personification to its opposite, especially when man no longer sees himself as the center of world events and is satisfied with a more meager CONCRETIZATION, with the recognition of causally acting forces of nature as the image of highest strength. INDIVIDUAL PSYCHOLOGY . . . would by the essence of its view be forced to regard such an unpremised, mechanistic view as an illusion inasmuch as it is without GOAL and direction, just like drive psychology, which is cut from the same cloth (Adler, 1979, p. 277).

See Adler, 1979, "Religion and Individual Psychology," pp. 271-308; Powers, R. L., (2003).

GOLD MINE

The use of the term **gold mine** in counseling and psychotherapy was introduced by Dreikurs, who taught his students to attend to a remark made naively by a client that, with appropriate inquiry as to the client's meaning when using it, might yield riches in understanding the client's MOVEMENT. Dreikurs told students to "start digging" when they suspected a **gold mine**. Grunwald and McAbee (1999) provide examples of **gold mines** (pp. 72-73), and define the **gold mine** as follows:

> **Gold mines** are words or phrases that imply a broader meaning, an underlying attitude, or a strong FEELING that influences the client's behavior (Grunwald & McAbee, 1999, p. 72).

GROUP THERAPY/MULTIPLE THERAPY

Some have said that Adler originated **group therapy** in Vienna in 1920, when he began counseling children, teachers, and families in the presence of the larger group of persons interested in the problems that disturb their relationships. Issues that had previously been private matters were now discussed among others for the first time (Ganz, 1953, p. 109). Though Adler did not practice **group therapy** as it is known today, he suggested **group treatment** of criminals, saying, "While I do not believe it would be possible to give every criminal an individual treatment, we could contribute much by **group treatment**," going on to discuss the kinds of work that could be done in such a **group**, and predicting that "we could achieve great results" (p. 348). Terner and Pew (1978) report that Dreikurs introduced **group therapy** into his private practice in 1928, and was probably the first psychiatrist to do so (p. 78). [See OPEN FORUM FAMILY COUNSELING/COMMUNITY CHILD GUIDANCE CENTERS.]

Multiple therapy (or co-therapy) refers to the involvement of more than one therapist in a case. It is not uncommon for two therapists to work together with a client in the process of LIFESTYLE ASSESSMENT, and a co-therapist team made up of male and female partners can be particularly valuable in couple and marriage counseling and therapy. In **group therapy**, while it is typical for one therapist to facilitate the group, two can enrich the experience, and the presence of two leaders can allow for the formation of sub-groups at particular times. A number of Adlerian practitioners have addressed the uses and processes of **multiple** and **group therapy**.

For **Group Therapy**, see Carlson, J., Watts, R. E., & Maniacci, M. P. (2006); Dinkmeyer, D. C. Jr., & Sperry, L. (2000); Manaster, G. J. & Corsini, R. J. (1982); and Sonstegard, M. A. & Bitter, J. R. (with Pelonis, P.) (2004).

For **Multiple Therapy**, see Dreikurs, R., Shulman, B. H., & Mosak, H. H. (1984); Powers, R. L. & Griffith, J. (1987).

GUESSING METHOD/STOCHASTIC METHOD

Conjecture, or educated **guessing**, is used to narrow the field of probability in order to uncover the GOAL of client MOVEMENT. The term "**stochastic method**" is derived from the Greek, *stokhazesthai*, meaning to aim at, to guess at, in order to hit a target (*stochos*). The **guessing method** as Adler practiced it is a way to approach an UNDERSTANDING of the hidden and PRIVATE SENSE of the NEUROTIC client or MISBEHAVING CHILD. Adler's avoidance of abstruse scientific terms and his elevation of common language in all his expressions is illustrated here. He saw **guessing** as the basis for intuition, admiring the intuitive achievements of poets and other artists in the portrayal of character. He also recognized **guessing** as a commonplace, noting that "everyone makes use of it constantly in the chaos of life, before the abysmal uncertainty of the future" (p. 329).

Because each of us operates out of unexamined assumptions and convictions, no one of us knows the truth about another, and because INDIVIDUAL PSYCHOLOGY is a subjective psychology, we can claim no objective truth about a person apart from his or her own opinions and attitudes. The client is sovereign as concerns his or her own life. Adler and Dreikurs recommended offering suggestions in the form of questions or tentative hypotheses, such as "Could it be. . . ?" If in response there is a RECOGNITION REFLEX, client and counselor have an opening to explore further. The therapist may also offer line-by-line **guesses** or hypotheses in the process of the interview. This approach to understanding — **guessing**, followed by the corrective of the client's reflexes and responses — is known formally as the **stochastic method**.

> Correct **guessing** is the first step toward the mastery of our problems (p. 329).

> In all . . . [your] explanations and interpretations you have to use your experience, you have to use INDIVIDUAL PSYCHOLOGICAL views, and you have *to guess* (Adler, 1979, p. 145).

> You have to *guess* but you have to prove it by other signs which agree. If you have **guessed** and the other signs do not agree, you have to be hard and cruel enough against yourself to look for another explanation (Adler, 1979, p. 162).

> Correct **guessing** distinguishes especially the man who is a partner, a fellow man, and [who] is interested in the successful solution of all human problems (p. 329).

> Truth will sooner come out from ERROR than from confusion (Bacon, F., 1620, Aphorism 20, Book II).

GUIDING LINES

Adler used the term **guiding lines** in several contexts to conceptualize the psychological construction of an orientation for MOVEMENT. The **guiding lines** are to be thought of as analogous to meridian lines on a map, not drawn on the surface of the earth in reality, but constructed as conventional devices necessary to the charting of a course, for orientation. The psychological **guiding lines** are part of the person's PRIVATE SENSE, and are not required to be present in CONSCIOUSNESS. They are elements of those generally unexamined convictions and REHEARSED operations which shape the person's STYLE OF LIVING. They can be uncovered and re-evaluated through LIFE-STYLE assessment, and especially the examination of EARLY RECOLLECTIONS.

> In the soul of the child, a **guiding line** forms which urges toward the enhancement of the SELF-ESTEEM in order to escape insecurity (p. 99).

> A character trait is comparable to a **guiding line** which is attached to the individual as a pattern, permitting him to express his self-consistent personality in any situation without much reflection (p. 219).

> What we call *character* is the always repeated way, the **guiding line**, the way in which one behaves toward the problems of life on the strength on one's STYLE OF LIFE (p. 279).

> Every one of the abstract **guiding lines** . . . can be or can become available to consciousness in the form of a memory image [EARLY RECOLLECTIONS] (p. 288).

GUILT FEELINGS/GUILT COMPLEX

Guilt feelings are experienced and expressed AS IF they were serious judgments imposed upon oneself of moral failure or short-coming. Their meaning can be understood in their consequences, which are to stall and provide a substitute in place of forward MOVEMENT and CONTRIBUTION on THE USEFUL SIDE OF LIFE, while at the same time SAFEGUARDING one's FEELINGS of self-worth and SUPERIORITY. The statement, "I **feel guilty** *because* I don't do what I know I should do," can be translated into, "I **feel guilty** *instead* of doing what I know I should do." This veils the individual's retreat from useful participation. Another statement, "I am **guilty** of the same faults I see in others," should be seen as including a HIDDEN MEANING, "but at least I have the decency to admit it." **Guilt feelings** and their **complex** of deception, pretense, and hidden claims to SUPERIORITY differ from contrition, which is an acceptance of responsibility for past ERRORS, combined with a readiness to make restitution where possible, and an intention to use any present opportunity to behave more honestly, usefully, and COOPERATIVELY in the present situation.

Of a patient obsessed by **guilt feelings** who prostrated himself and shouted to a large congregation at church, "I am the greatest sinner of all men!", Adler said, "His **feelings of guilt** were [the] means to make him appear more honest than others and in this way he was struggling to achieve SUPERIORITY" (Adler, 1980, p. 33). In another instance, illustrating Adler's way of reducing the dramatic power of a disturbance, a young man confessed, "I masturbate, and I **feel guilty**," to which Adler replied, "You masturbate *and* **feel guilty**? It's too much. *Either* masturbate *or* **feel guilty**" (K. A. Adler, personal communication, n. d.). [SEE HESITATING ATTITUDE/DISTANCING.]

> Preference for the hinterland of life is notably SAFEGUARDED by the individual's mode of thinking and argumentation, occasionally also by COMPULSIVE thinking or by fruitless **guilt feelings** (p. 273).

> In the majority of NEUROTIC cases the fact is that a **guilt complex** is used as a means to fix its maker on THE USELESS SIDE OF LIFE (p. 272).

HEREDITY (GENETIC POSSIBILITY)/ENVIRONMENT (ENVIRONMENTAL OPPORTUNITY)

The nature vs. nurture controversy, originally the name of a religious dispute in an early 19th Century New England church over the meaning of original sin (Ahlstrom, 1972, pp. 610-611), continues to haunt popular and scientific thinking with an added new name, **heredity** vs. **environment**. Opinion shifts between **genetic** material as fixed, but not necessarily expressed, and **environmental** influences as fluid, and not necessarily impacting in any particular. For INDIVIDUAL PSYCHOLOGY, all questions of what one has (assuming a PSYCHOLOGY OF POSSESSION), such as certain **genetic** material or a certain childhood history, are distilled into Adler's question: "*Who* uses it?", reflecting a PSYCHOLOGY OF USE (p. 176).

Powers and Griffith (1987) state that the individual's opinion of self in childhood includes considerations of **genetic possibility** in the realms of physical and mental capacities, and DEGREE OF ACTIVITY, that lead to a self-assessment [SELF-CONCEPT] that could be expressed, "These are my personal limits and possibilities for MAKING A PLACE amongst others." At the same time, the child is aware of his or her situation in life, and evaluates **environmental opportunities** as openings for advancement, as if to say, "This is what is open to me in life, and this is what stands in my way" (p. 25). [See SELF-ESTEEM/SELF CONCEPT; LIFESTYLE.]

> The raw material with which the INDIVIDUAL PSYCHOLOGIST works is: The *relationship* of the individual to the problems of the outside world. The INDIVIDUAL PSYCHOLOGIST has to observe how a particular individual relates himself to the outside world. This outside world includes the individual's own body, his bodily functions, and the functions of his mind. He does not relate himself to the outside world in a predetermined manner as is often assumed. He relates himself always according to his own interpretation of himself and of his present problem. His limits are not only the common human limits, but also the limits he has set himself. It is neither **heredity** nor **environment** that determines his relationship to the outside world. **Heredity** only endows him with certain abilities. **Environment** only gives him certain impressions. These abilities and impressions, and the manner in which he "experiences" them — that is to say, the interpretation he makes of these experiences — are the bricks that he uses in his own "CREATIVE" way to build up his attitude toward life. It is his individual way of using these bricks — or in other words, it is his attitude toward life — that determines his relationship to the outside world (Adler, 1935, p. 5).

HESITATING ATTITUDE/DISTANCING

Hesitation is one of four "distancing" maneuvers Adler identified as SAFEGUARDING devices; the others are moving backward, standing still, and the construction of obstacles (pp. 273-276). Adler regarded **hesitation** as a sign of a person's diminished courage to do what the situation requires. It may show itself in a variety of ways: in laziness ("Laziness indicates the **hesitating attitude**. We can deduce from it that the child no longer believes that he can advance" [p. 391]); in misbehavior ("There is only one reason for an individual to side-step to THE USELESS SIDE: the fear of a defeat on THE USEFUL SIDE" [p. 157]); in depression ("INDIVIDUAL PSYCHOLOGY sees in this type the pronouncedly **hesitating** individual who does not have the confidence to overcome difficulties and to advance, but who initiates his further steps with the greatest caution and who prefers to stand still or to turn back rather that to take any risk" [p. 170]). The idea of **hesitation** is not to be confused with or mistaken for the psychoanalytic concepts of *ambivalence* or *intrapsychic conflict,* here seen as rationalizations offered as excuses to account for the failure of COURAGE expressed in **hesitation**. [See COMPULSION/COUNTER-COMPULSION.]

> The essential tendency of the NEUROTIC is the STRIVING from the FEELING OF INFERIORITY toward "above". . . . The resultant combination . . . [is] a NEUROTIC constant back-and-forth, a half- and-half (p. 273).

> This peculiar process is demonstrable in all NEUROSES and PSYCHOSES, and has been described by me in detail as the **"hesitating attitude"** (p. 273).

> The patient never deviates from the road of evasion, which he paves with good intentions or feelings of GUILT. "Conflict" only means a standstill (p. 307).

> If an individual cannot decide whether he should do this or do that, one thing is certain, namely, that he does not move (Adler, 1979, p. 93).

HIDDEN MEANING/HIDDEN REASON

Toward the very end of his life, Dreikurs began to speak of the **hidden reason**, with some urgency, as the name for something he felt he had discovered, and which represented a way of understanding particular behaviors of an otherwise puzzling kind. In fact it appears that he may have rediscovered this idea, in his memory of things he had learned from Adler, to whom he was always willing to defer as the one from whom he had learned his ways of understanding, renaming it in line with the ways he had encountered it in clinical experience.

> This goal [of the individual] enables us to understand the **hidden meaning** behind the various separate acts and to see them as parts of a whole. Vice versa when we study the parts, provided we study them as parts of a whole, we get a better sense of the whole (pp. 92-93).

HISTORICAL CONTEXT: ADLER IN HIS TIME

Adler, as anyone, must be considered in the **context** of his time. Adler's time began in 1870 when he was born, the second son of a Jewish merchant in Vienna, the imperial city of Austro-Hungary, in the reign of Emperor Franz Josef. It was a time when Jews were tolerated but not yet citizens. Goods imported from the East were delivered by camel train. In the same year, Lenin, Jan Smuts (see Smuts, 1961), and Maria Montessori were born, Robert E. Lee died, and the Vatican Council proclaimed the infallibility of the Pope. Electric lights, telephones, automobiles, and airplanes were yet to come. In *The Story of Psychology* Hunt (1993) notes that, according to most historians, psychology was born in 1879, when Wilhelm Wundt conducted an APPERCEPTION experiment at the University of Leipzig. Adler was nine years old, to grow up in the era of the new field, which he later entered with many of his peers. He became a pioneer in efforts to employ scientific method and the discipline of medical study to UNDERSTAND human behavior. The mystery of SEXUALITY, an important part of the study, was being conducted by men in an era of virtually unchallenged male domination, and all that this implies for cooperation (and its failures) between the sexes.

Royal families ruled almost all the people on earth. The ruling class had ruthlessly crushed the revolutions of 1848 and maintained their positions with increasing force and oppression. Many looked back to a "quieter" time when subject peoples knew who their betters were and accepted their positions of INFERIORITY. Others looked forward, including many women of the nascent FEMINIST movement, and pressed for social justice. Adler joined the reformers of the Socialist Party. He graduated from medical school, married, opened a practice, began his family of four children, and in 1902 joined Freud's famous "Wednesdays" (see AGGRESSION). In 1904 he was baptized, together with two of his children. His first book, on psychosomatics, was published in 1907; in 1912 he published *The Neurotic Character,* an exposition establishing the independence of his psychological theory (Stein, 2002). After his departure from Freud's circle in 1911, he and those sympathetic to his new approach developed the theory and practice of INDIVIDUAL PSYCHOLOGY.

World War I challenged the idea of progress across Europe amidst the horrors of poison gas, trench warfare, and machine-gun fire. Adler, drafted to serve as a physician, not only worked to preserve lives but also maneuvered to keep damaged men from being returned to the Front. Post-war saw the collapse of the Hapsburgs in Austro-Hungary, the Hohenzollerns in Germany (with the abdication of the Kaiser), the Romanoff dynasty in Russia, and the Osmanlis in Turkey and its former dominions in the Middle East, and the domestication of the remaining European monarchs. The ensuing turbulence and social change, led to despair among many who mourned the loss of the old order; among others there was an awareness of new and better possibility.

INDIVIDUAL PSYCHOLOGY thrived from the post-World War I period until Adler's death. He practiced, organized the Vienna child guidance centers, lectured, taught, wrote, traveled to France, the United Kingdom, the United States and elsewhere, and by these means made himself and the theory known. In 1929 he began a lectureship at Columbia University, New York, after which he spent parts of each year in the United States, planning to emigrate when it would be possible financially and convenient for the family.

But the world intervened. Austrian fascists following the lead of the rising Nazis in Germany, closed the child guidance clinics, and Jews were fired and harassed. By 1934 Adler determined to move his family to the safety of New York; his cherished first-born daughter Valentina, with her husband, fled to Russia, her mother's homeland. Their hope — not uncommon then among idealists — was to contribute to democracy and the making of the "New Man" there. Only three months before a lecture tour in Holland and the United Kingdom began, Adler's letters and wires to Valentina were returned marked: "Not At this Address." Efforts to reach her were of no avail. In May of 1937, at 67, Adler died of heart failure in Aberdeen, Scotland after completing four days of lectures at the Medical College. After the war his family learned that Valentina had perished in Stalin's gulag.

In this **context**, Adler's concepts of INDIVIDUAL PSYCHOLOGY arose. It was a world of man above and woman below, INFERIORITY FEELINGS and SUPERIORITY STRIVING, a world craving UNDERSTANDING of human ERROR, of personal responsibility in the creation of LIFESTYLE, and, above all else, of COURAGE and the COMPENSATORY solace and hope inherent in COMMUNITY FEELING.

HOLISM

Holism posits the idea that the whole is greater than the sum of its parts and that, unified, the parts constitute a new and UNIQUE whole. The term is from the Greek, *holos*, meaning whole, and was coined by Jan Smuts (1870-1950) in his book, *Holism and Evolution* (1926/1961). Adler corresponded with Smuts, and had Smuts's book translated into German for the use of his students. Holistic Psychology would have been an apt name for Adler's approach. However, prior to the publication of Smuts's text, and before the term **holism** had entered into common currency, Adler had already chosen the name *Individualpsychologie,* for his "science for the understanding of persons" (G., *Menschenkenntnis*). Based on the Latin, *individuum* (that which cannot be divided; indivisible), Adler's term emphasized the contrast between his approach and Freud's psychoanalysis. Freud, by analogy to the chemist's analysis of a substance into its constituent elements (Gr., *analuein* = to break up, cut apart), had suggested an analytic breakdown of the psyche into its supposed parts.

In the later history of modern psychology, **holism** came to represent the view of persons emerging in their developments as organic unities, and of a person's thoughts, feelings, and actions as self-consistent behaviors expressive of one indivisible and UNIQUE VARIANT of human possibility. This is entirely congruent with INDIVIDUAL PSYCHOLOGY, which may be said to carry the idea of indivisibility even further by explicitly rejecting the image of personal SELFBOUNDEDNESS (G., *ICHGEBUNDENHEIT*) in favor of the person's indivisible EMBEDDEDNESS in his or her social and historical situation.

> One can never regard single manifestations of the mental life as separate entities, but . . . one can gain UNDERSTANDING of them only if one UNDERSTANDS all manifestations of a mental life as parts of an indivisible whole (p. 190).

> With every individual, we must look below the surface. We must look for the underlying coherence, for the unity of the personality. This unity is fixed in all its expressions (p. 189).

> Something new can never be created through analysis. Here we would have parts in our hands instead of the whole. To us INDIVIDUAL PSYCHOLOGISTS, the whole tells much more than the analysis of the parts. Also, nothing new can emerge through synthesis if one simply puts the parts together (Adler, 1964b, p. 30).

> In all probability, the mind governs and influences the whole building up of the body (p. 225).

> Everything is in anything (R. L. Powers, personal communication, n.d.).

HORIZONTAL vs. VERTICAL PLANES OF MOVEMENT

The terms **horizontal** and **vertical planes of movement** were introduced by Lydia Sicher in a paper presented at the 1954 Annual Meeting of the American Society of Adlerian Psychology (published in 1955, see below) to illustrate Adler's concepts of (a) STRIVING for SUPERIORITY in line with the SOCIAL INTEREST and (b) STRIVING for *personal* SUPERIORITY. **Horizontal movement** evokes an image of task-centered, egalitarian problem-solving. The question governing **horizontal movement** is, "What does the situation require?" In contrast, **vertical movement** is the pursuit of prestige and status, focused on a GOAL of self-elevation. Questions governing **vertical movement** are, "How am I doing?", "How do I look?" **Horizontal movement** proceeds on the strength of confidence in the processes of growth, development, and solidarity with others, minimizing contentiousness and competitive STRIVING. **Vertical movement** proceeds from SAFEGUARDING attitudes and isolating ambitions of "getting ahead" so as not to be "falling behind" others, AS IF in a struggle for limited resources, minimizing the values of BELONGINGNESS and feelings of mutual respect and engagement. [See COMMUNITY FEELING/SOCIAL FEELING/SOCIAL INTEREST.]

> When individuals . . . feel weak, they cease to be interested socially but strive for [PERSONAL] SUPERIORITY. They want to solve the problems of life in such a way as to obtain PERSONAL SUPERIORITY without any admixture of SOCIAL INTEREST (p. 260).

> The idea of living on a **vertical plane** is . . . perhaps the most neuroticizing element of all [in a child's development]. Yet so much of the TRAINING of children is based on it: Hitch your wagon to the stars! The sky is the limit! Don't let anyone keep you down! You have to be better, more, than the next [person] (Sicher, 1955, p. 100).

> Substituting the **horizontal** for the **vertical plane** of life changes the aspect completely. Here the ideas of SUPERIOR and INFERIOR have no place. . . . The **horizontal plane** affords the possibility of developing one's potentialities within the world of one's fellow men; it alone allows for the dynamic forging ahead of one and all (Sicher, 1955, p. 101).

> [In **horizontal movement**] the desire to be USEFUL can never be frustrated. . . . Self-fulfillment no longer depends on what others think or do, but on what one can CONTRIBUTE. Concern with status is unnecessary, since one can be sure of ONE'S PLACE in the group as an equal (Dreikurs, 1973, p. 41).

> The **vertical movement** of self-elevation, regardless of the height it leads to, both in status and accomplishments, can never bring lasting satisfaction and inner peace. There is a constant danger of falling and failing; the gnawing feeling of real or possible INFERIORITY is never eradicated, regardless of success (Dreikurs, 1973, p. 41).

> In view of these obvious consequences of a mistake-centered orientation, why is it then maintained? Two possible reasons seem evident. One is a vestige from an outgrown autocratic society. In such a society, doing wrong means not doing what one is supposed to do, and this is intolerable, as a defiance of authority. . . . [A second cause] . . . lies in the competitive strife on the **vertical plane**. Making a mistake . . . lowers one's social status, as being right increases it. . . . Once we free ourselves from our fear of being INFERIOR and recognize our worth and dignity, we no longer fear making mistakes — and therefore make fewer. This is learned in psychotherapy. Our educational institutions are not yet prepared to teach this new social value of THE COURAGE TO BE IMPERFECT (Dreikurs, 1973, p. 43).

INDIVIDUAL PSYCHOLOGY/ADLERIAN PSYCHOLOGY

From 1902 Adler was a leading participant in the circle of physicians and others who gathered to form the Vienna Psychoanalytic Society at the invitation of the founder of the group, Sigmund Freud. His relationship with Freud, whom he served as confidant and personal physician, was especially close. Later, as the Society took on a more formal character, Adler became its first president, and the co-editor of its first journal. By 1911, however, it was apparent that Adler's theoretical development was moving in ways that were not congruent with Freud's ideas. Early in 1911 Adler was asked to present a series of papers over the course of three successive meetings of the Society, for the purpose of detailing and formally setting forth the lines of his developing theoretical distinctions. These were especially those referred to under the term, "MASCULINE PROTEST," which more and more clearly could be seen as a challenge, if not a refutation of Freud's "libido" theory. The consequent division that showed itself in the discussions that followed, while it was for the most part expressed in the polite language of scientific debate, was clearly acrimonious, and the differences between the two most important figures in the Society very quickly came to be seen as irreconcilable. Adler took the initiative, voluntarily resigned as co-editor of the journal and president of the Society, with about one third of the members, who began to meet with him in a separate group, which they called "The Society for Free Psychoanalytic Research."

The name was unmistakably pejorative. Within a short time Freud decreed that those who took part in the proceedings of the new group were no longer welcome at meetings of the original group. Adler had by this time begun to call his method "Comparative **Individual Psychology**," to give emphasis to (a) each person as a UNIQUE VARIANT of human possibility in his or her style of approaching the problems of social living (*Comparative*); (b) the UNITY of the organism and the personality as an indivisible whole, indivisibly EMBEDDED in a social and historical situation (*Individual*); and (c) the agency of the person, a "soul" to be understood by a focus on PURPOSE, not process (*Psychology*). Before long therefore, the new group took the name **Individual Psychology** Society, to underscore these emphases, which the German name was able to achieve in the single word, ***Individualpsychologie.*** The English name, necessitating two words for its translation, has been misinterpreted as if it were meant to emphasize the identification and study of the individual in isolation from his or her social CONTEXT, an unfortunate and unintended deformity of Adler's meaning. Probably for this reason, among others, Adler's work has come to be more commonly known under the name **Adlerian Psychology**. [See COMMUNITY FEELING/ SOCIAL FEELING/SOCIAL INTEREST; HOLISM; MASCULINE PROTEST; ORGAN INFERIORITY.]

> **Individual Psychology** is probably the most consistent theory of the position of the individual to the problems of social living, and is in this sense, therefore, social psychology (p. 157).

INDIVIDUAL VARIANT/UNIQUENESS

Throughout the development and practice of INDIVIDUAL PSYCHOLOGY, Adler stressed the UNIQUENESS of each person, thus introducing into psychology what was already known in other areas, and that since his time is more widely known, about **individual variants**, as (to give a prime example) in the **uniqueness** of each person's DNA profile. In order to gain a psychological UNDERSTANDING of another human being, he argued against thinking of persons in terms of TYPES. Instead he considered how this one person, in his or her own experience of childhood, created his or her way of being in the world, perceived and made use of GENETIC POSSIBILITY and ENVIRONMENTAL OPPORTUNITY, and rehearsed and refined his or her idiosyncratic LAW OF MOVEMENT. An individual attitude toward self, others, and the world unmistakably identifies this one UNIQUE person. [See TYPES/TENDENCIES/THEMES/PRIORITIES.]

In recent years those who want to stress the importance of biological inheritance over individual choice and creativity have focused on the life patterns of identical twins, including those separated in childhood and raised separately. Many striking similarities are noted, including indications of identical preferences in matters of taste and personal choice. Apart from the necessarily subjective character of such studies, there are certain hard statistical measurements that argue against the genetic determinism they purport to demonstrate. Dr. Atul Gawande (2007) of the Harvard Medical School, in a recent essay reported that "genetically identical twins vary widely in life span: the typical gap is more than fifteen years" (p. 52).[2]

> Each individual always manifests himself as **unique**, be it in thinking, feeling, speaking, or acting (p. 194).

> Everything can also be different (*Alles kann auch anders sein*. The **uniqueness** of the individual cannot be expressed in a short formula, and general rules — even those laid down by INDIVIDUAL PSYCHOLOGY, of my own creation — should be regarded as nothing more than an aid to a preliminary illumination of the FIELD of view in which the single individual can be found — or missed (p. 194).

> It has been imputed to us that we assume and strive for the sameness of men. This is a myth. Quite on the contrary, we attempt to examine the nuances, the **uniqueness** of the GOAL, the **uniqueness** of the opinion of a man of himself and the TASKS OF LIFE. The task of INDIVIDUAL PSYCHOLOGY is to comprehend the **individual variant** (p. 180).

> [INDIVIDUAL PSYCHOLOGY] attempts to gain, from the separate life manifestations and forms of expression the picture of the self-consistent personality as a **variant**, by presupposing the UNITY (G., *Einheit*) and self-consistency of the individuality (p. 179).

INFERIORITY COMPLEX

Inferiority complex is a term attributed to and adopted by Adler though, according to H. L. and R. R. Ansbacher (p. 256), probably not originating with him. It refers to those FEELINGS OF INFERIORITY which are experienced as *personal* deficiencies as opposed to the *universal* sense of incompleteness. As such they may come to be felt as so overwhelming that they undermine the COURAGE to move forward with life, to meet and overcome obstacles, and to develop oneself and make a CONTRIBUTION to the community. The term **inferiority complex** applies when INFERIORITY FEELINGS cease to be a spur to further growth and become themselves a rationale for a HESITATING ATTITUDE. [As elsewhere in this text, note the distinction between two meanings of the word *FEELING*: one is affect, EMOTION; the other (as here) apprehension, sense of things.]

It is not the SENSE OF INFERIORITY which matters but the degree and character of it (p. 257).

The abnormal FEELING OF INFERIORITY has acquired the name **'inferiority complex'** (p. 257).

It is more than a complex; it is almost a disease (p. 257).

[INFERIORITY FEELING] becomes a pathological condition only when the sense of inadequacy overwhelms the individual and, far from stimulating him to useful activity, makes him depressed and incapable of development (p. 258).

The **inferiority complex** is the presentation of the person to himself and others that he is not strong enough to solve a given problem in a socially useful way (p. 258).

The **inferiority complex**, that is, the persistence of the consequences of the FEELING OF INFERIORITY and the retention of that feeling, finds its explanation in greater lack of SOCIAL INTEREST (p. 258).

We say that a person is suffering from an **"inferiority complex"** when he reacts fatalistically to a crippling situation, real or fancied, without attempting to correct or improve it (Adler, Alexandra, 1971, p. 3).

The **"inferiority complex"** does not lead to any compensation. It is a deadlock for any further development (Dreikurs, 1973, p. 180).

The **inferiority complex** involves an appeal to INFERIORITY FEELINGS, as if in themselves they constituted a handicap, and so may be offered as an excuse from participation and contribution. In fact, in the "complex" they are rehearsed and made to serve as a disguise for loss of COURAGE, or an alibi for failure (B. H. Shulman, personal communication, n.d.).

INFERIORITY FEELINGS

Inferiority feelings (G., *Minderwertigkeitsgefühl*) are those universal human feelings of incompleteness, smallness, weakness, ignorance, and dependency included in our first experiences of ourselves in infancy and early childhood. **Inferiority feelings** continue to be experienced to greater or lesser degree throughout adult life. For the well-adapted individual, whose sense of solidarity and belonging among others is cultivated by education and ENCOURAGEMENT, these feelings serve as spurs to effort and as a source of motivation to overcome obstacles, to grow, and to improve oneself and the community. [Note that the word *feelings* in this formulation is not to be understood as equivalent to EMOTION, as used otherwise. Here it refers to a *sense* of things, a contact with underlying reality, prior to biased opinion, perhaps by analogy to "sea legs" for one accustomed to the *sense* of being on board a moving vessel.] [See EXISTENTIALISM.]

To be human means **to feel inferior** (p. 115).

Every child is actually **inferior** in the face of life and could not exist at all without a considerable measure of SOCIAL INTEREST on the part of those close to him (p. 115).

At the beginning of every psychological life there is a more or less deep **inferiority feeling** (p. 115).

To be a human being means to possess a **feeling of inferiority** which constantly presses toward its own conquest (p. 116).

The **inferiority feeling** dominates the psychological life and can easily be understood from the FEELING of imperfection and of incompletion and from the incessant STRIVING of man and mankind (pp. 116-117).

Inferiority feelings are not in themselves ABNORMAL. They are the cause of all improvements in the position of mankind (p. 117).

Human beings are in a permanent mood of **inferiority feeling**, which constantly spurs them on to attain greater security (p. 123).

IRON LOGIC OF COMMUNAL LIFE

H. L. and R. R. Ansbacher identify the "**iron logic of communal life**" as Adler's phrase to convey recognition of the fact that human beings are embedded "in a larger whole" (p. 127), and that the experience of life itself makes demands upon the individual which form the "absolute truth" of human experience.

> The demands of society have regulated human relations which had already existed from the beginning as self-understood, as an absolute truth (p. 128).

> Before the individual life of man there was the community (p. 128).

> Human psychological life is not capable of doing just as it likes but is constantly confronted with TASKS which have arrived from somewhere. All these tasks are inseparably tied up with the **logic of man's communal life** (p. 128).

> [If we know the GOAL of a person] we could perhaps determine that his GOAL is too far removed . . . from the **absolute logic of human communal life** (p.196).

> The common people seem always to have been on the track to SOCIAL INTEREST, and every intellectual and religious uprising has been directed against the STRIVING for power; **the logic of the communal life of man** has always asserted itself. But all this has always ended again in the thirst for dominance (pp. 455-456).

LIFE-STYLE ASSESSMENT/LIFE-STYLE DIAGNOSIS

The **life-style assessment** or **life-style diagnosis** is a structured inquiry into and interpretation of an individual's UNIQUE STYLE OF LIVING. It is a major psychological **assessment** tool of Adlerian-trained therapists, combining the elements of psychotherapeutic confrontation, challenge, and GUIDANCE toward reorientation with diagnosis. The modern **assessment** inquiry is generally organized in two parts: (a) The FAMILY CONSTELLATION, which includes FAMILY ATMOSPHERE AND VALUES, parental relationship, GENDER GUIDING LINES, PSYCHOLOGICAL BIRTH-ORDER VANTAGE and sibling relationships, and the challenge of ADOLESCENCE and gender identity; (b) the EARLY RECOLLECTIONS. The **assessment** interpretations may include three summaries: (a) The summary of the FAMILY CONSTELLATION; (b) the pattern of basic convictions (derived from an interpretation of the EARLY RECOLLECTIONS); and (c) an enumeration of BASIC MISTAKES or INTERFERING IDEAS. [See SIBLING RIVALRY (COMPETITION).]

> According to my experience, so far the most trustworthy approaches to the exploration of personality are given in a comprehensive UNDERSTANDING of (1) the EARLIEST CHILDHOOD RECOLLECTIONS, (2) the position of the child in the BIRTH-ORDER, (3) childhood disorders [ORGAN INFERIORITY; OVERBURDENING CHILDHOOD SITUATIONS], (4) day and night DREAMS, and (5) the nature of the EXOGENOUS FACTOR that causes the illness (pp. 327-328).

> In a way we are like archeologists who find fragments of earthenware, tools, the ruined walls of buildings, broken monuments, and leaves of papyrus; and from these fragments proceed to infer the life of a whole city which has perished. Only we are dealing . . . with the inter-organized aspects of a human being, a living personality which can continuously set before us new manifestations of its own meaning (p. 332).

For **life-style assessment** guides, see Adler's original "Interview Guides" (pp. 404-409); Dreikurs, R. (1967), "Guide for Initial Interviews Establishing the Life Style," pp. 88-90; Eckstein, D., Baruth, L., & Mahrer, D. (1982); Powers, R. L. & Griffith, J. (1995); Shulman, B. H., & Mosak, H. H. (1988).

LIFE-STYLE/LIFESTYLE/STYLE OF LIVING/STYLE OF LIFE

The **style of living** or **lifestyle** is the unique and self-consistent UNITY in MOVEMENT (thought, FEELING, action) of the individual, created in early childhood[3] in the CONTEXT of GENETIC POSSIBILITY and ENVIRONMENTAL OPPORTUNITY (SOFT DETERMINISM), organized and given direction by the subjectively conceived GOAL, based upon GUIDING FICTIONS and following GUIDING LINES that are relied upon and reinforced through TRAINING, SELF-TRAINING, AND THE REHEARSAL OF CHARACTER.

In INDIVIDUAL PSYCHOLOGY **lifestyle** is congruent with the term personality in other psychological systems, but is contrasted to them not least because of its emphasis on the person's characteristic way of MOVEMENT. Adler first used the too-easily reified and misunderstood term *life plan*. He abandoned this phrase at the suggestion of a student (who previously had studied with sociologist Max Weber) in favor of Weber's phrase **life-style**. The new phrase was better able to convey Adler's sense of the CREATIVE, artistic side of the development of the unique individual. (Unfortunately, also, it has never lost its association to Weber's meaning of a characteristic set of values and practices associated with a social class; this gives rise to confusion as to its meaning in Adler's use of it.) In INDIVIDUAL PSYCHOLOGY the **style of living** is meant, in brief, to refer to (a) the person's characteristic way of operating in the social field; (b) the basic convictions concerning self, others, and the world actively maintained in the person's schema of BIASED APPERCEPTION; and (c) the person's self-created GOAL of perfection, or SELF IDEAL.

> The **style of life** . . . is developed in earliest childhood (p. 186).

> [The child's] opinion of life, which is at the bottom of his attitude to life and is neither shaped into words nor expressed in thought, is his own masterpiece. Thus the child arrives at his LAW OF MOVEMENT which aids him after a certain amount of TRAINING to obtain a **style of life**, in accordance with which we see the individual thinking, FEELING, and acting throughout his whole life (pp. 187-188).

> The **style of life** commands all forms of expression; the whole commands the parts. . . . The foremost task of INDIVIDUAL PSYCHOLOGY is to prove this UNITY in each individual — in his thinking, FEELING, acting, in his so-called CONSCIOUS and UNCONSCIOUS, in every expression of his personality. This UNITY we call the **style of life** of the individual (p. 175).

> The **style of life** of an individual is wholly accomplished in earliest childhood and is not changed so long as the individual does not UNDERSTAND the unavoidable discrepancies [of his style] regarding the inescapable demands of social problems (p. 192).

> Anything that is not palatable to the **style of life** is rejected, forgotten, or saved as a warning example. The **style of life** decides (p. 213).

> [For] Adler, the construction of the "**life style**" is completed by the individual at about the age of four or five. His interpretations of what life is, what he is, what others are and what his relationships to others mean, is pretty nearly fixed by that age, and forms his total attitudes to life in all situations. New experiences are, from that time on, interpreted only from the point of view of his **life style**. This results in a biased selection of perceptions, with the exclusion, or at least depreciation, of all those experiences that do not fit his style of life. All thinking, FEELING and acting of an individual support his **style of life**. Thoughts, FEELINGS and actions that would undermine or contradict his **life style** are largely rejected (K. A. Adler, p. iv, Introduction, Adler, 1963).

For a report and discussion of the *Kern Lifestyle Scale* (1997) and the expanded version, BASIS-A (Basic Adlerian Scales for Inter-personal Success [1993]), by Kern, R. M., Wheeler, J., and Curlette, W., see Dinkmeyer, D., Jr. & Sperry, L. (2000), pp. 303-306.

LIFE TASKS

Using the image of a teacher who sets assignments (G., *Aufgabe*) for students, Adler observed that, by virtue of being born, each human being is confronted by three unavoidable **tasks**. These are (a) **the social task** of living as one amongst others: "We have always to reckon with others" (p. 132), since we are born into a world of others, who are affected by our entering it and by everything we choose or refuse to do in it, and on whose good will and comradeship we depend for our very existence; (b) **the work task**: Our continuing to live "on this poor earth crust" (p. 155), made possible by the work of others, demands that we offer something in exchange; (c) **the love task**: Since each human being lives as a "member of one of the two sexes and not of the other" (p. 132), he or she must meet the challenge of sexual COOPERATION, on which depends the future of humanity.[4] [See LOVE/COUPLES/MARRIAGE; MAKING/TAKING/FINDING A PLACE FOR ONESELF; HORIZONTAL VS. VERTICAL PLANES OF MOVEMENT.]

> Three problems are irrevocably set before every individual. These are: the attitude towards one's fellow man, occupation, and love. All three are linked with one another by the first. They are not accidental, but inescapable problems (p. 297).

> All the questions of life can be subordinated to the three major problems — the problems of communal life, of work, and of love (p. 131).

See Ferguson, E. D. (2007) for a discussion of Adlerian concepts applied to the workplace.

LOVE/COUPLES/MARRIAGE

Adler defined **love** with SEXUAL intimacy as one of the three TASKS OF LIFE that must be met by each person (see LIFE TASKS). The **love** TASK begins for children in the intimacy of breast-feeding (or its simulation, unavailable in Adler's day), which, Adler noted, is the child's first experience of COOPERATION. As the child develops, he or she gathers impressions (largely UNCONSCIOUS) of what it means to be a man or a woman, forms ideas about relationships between the sexes based on mother's and father's conjunctive or disjunctive MOVEMENT, and CONSCIOUSLY attends to other models of **love**, **coupleship**, and **marriage** (see GENDER GUIDING LINES AND ROLE MODELS).

If the child is encouraged, with EDUCATIONAL GUIDANCE informed by COMMUNITY FEELING, the child meets the challenges of ADOLESCENCE and SEXUALITY in all their complexity with COMMON SENSE and COURAGE. If the child is OVERBURDENED (see OVERBURDENING CHILDHOOD SITUATIONS), he or she will nonetheless seek means for OVERCOMING inevitable FEELINGS OF INFERIORITY. If the child is not ENCOURAGED and COMMUNITY FEELING is not fostered, these efforts may result in a HESITATING ATTITUDE, COMPULSIONS or other disorders, or worse, a hostile turning against others; any of these maladaptations brings with it unhappy consequences for the individual in meeting the task of love.

In our period, when COMPETITIVE and self-absorbed STRIVING is elevated as desirable, those who succeed in **coupleship** and **marriage** do so against the odds (as Adler points out in the quotations below). He offered a treasury of advice to his daughter, Valentina, and her husband upon their wedding. He wrote that living two-by-two, "is a task at which both of you must work, with joy"; he encouraged them to "live in such a way that you make the other's life easier and more beautiful," and cautioned, "Don't allow either of you to become subordinate to the other; no one can stand this attitude." He further advised, "Don't allow anyone else to gain influence over the shaping of your **marriage** relation," and "only make friends with people who have a sincere affection for you both" (Bottome, 1939, pp. 98-99).

> **Love** . . . is a TASK for two individuals. . . . To some degree we have been EDUCATED to work alone; to some degree, to work in a team or a group. We have generally had little experience of working two by two (Adler, 1982, p. 124).

> TRAINING has been too much toward individual success, toward considering what we can get out of life rather than what we can give to it. . . . [People] are unaccustomed to consulting another human being's interests and aims, desires, hopes, and ambitions. They are not prepared for the problems of a common TASK (Adler, 1982, pp. 125-126).

> In addition to physical suitability and attraction . . . [these points] are to be considered as indicators of a sufficient degree of SOCIAL INTEREST: (1) the partner must have proven he can maintain a friendship; (2) he must be interested in his work; (3) he must show more interest in his partner than in himself" (Adler, 1982, p. 325).

> **Love** is the equal partnership between a man and a woman where two are merged into one, a human dyad, reconciling the SEX urge with the biological needs of the race and the demands of society (Adler, 1982, p. 321).

> Some people are incapable of falling in **love** with one person. . . . They must fall in **love** with two at the same time. They thus feel free; they can escape from one to the other, and never undertake the full responsibilities of **love** (p. 437).

See Belove, L. (1980); Kern, R. M., Hawes, E. C., & Christensen, O. C. (1989); Sherman, R., & Feldman, N. (1986).

MAKING/TAKING/FINDING A PLACE FOR ONESELF

Making (or **taking**, or **finding**) **a place for oneself** is a phrase Dreikurs used, and is as distinctive as any in establishing the Adlerian way of studying the individual in his or her field of MOVEMENT. It opposes ideas of the person being shaped or determined by GENETIC endowment or ENVIRONMENTAL press, attending instead to the individual's efforts to establish and maintain a personally chosen social role. A claim to a **place** is first made and rehearsed by the child in the family of origin, and becomes the pattern of MOVEMENT that distinguishes oneself in social situations sought out and entered in subsequent development. An UNDERSTANDING of this active seeking and **taking a place** opposes ideas of outside influences too often supposed to be impressing themselves upon hapless and passive individuals. "Brains," "greasers," "jocks," and "nerds" (for example) do not either GUIDE or lead astray the adolescents who encounter them so much as they serve to provide reference groups in which the young person can see ways that are open to his or her **taking** and **making a place** for him- or herself in line with previously rehearsed stratagems. In summarizing a LIFE-STYLE ASSESSMENT therefore, the therapist will regularly state the **place** taken and held by each of the children in the family (following a pattern practiced and taught by Dreikurs).

> The patient [is asked] to elaborate spontaneously on his dissimilarities with his main competitor [among the siblings]; he describes each one's MOVEMENTS in their COMPETITIVE effort to **find a place** in the group. . . . Where one sibling succeeds, his competitor will give up every effort; where the other fails, he will move in. As a result, each becomes different from the other. Conversely, the siblings who are most alike are the allies (Dreikurs, 1973, p. 91).

> Earlier than we realize, children shape and mold themselves, their parents, and their environment. A child is an active and dynamic entity. He shares equally in establishing the relationships between himself and each other person in his environment. Each relationship is UNIQUE unto itself, depending entirely upon what each partner contributes to it. . . . Children develop their relationships to others through the use of their own CREATIVE POWERS and their ingenuity in trying to **find a place** (Dreikurs, 1964, pp. 32-33).

MASCULINE PROTEST

This is an important term, both in the history of modern psychology and in the history of Adler's theoretical development, especially in his momentous MOVEMENT from ideas of physical INFERIORITY and its psychical COMPENSATIONS toward considering personal opinions and FEELINGS of INFERIORITY as also giving rise to COMPENSATORY striving. The cultural assumptions of the social and sexual INFERIORITY of women, and the resistance to these assumptions mounted by socialist idealism and the demands of the Feminist Movement were powerful supports for his new way of thinking. As such they had a disruptive effect upon the discussions of the Vienna Psychoanalytic Society, of which Adler was now president. Adler argued that the presumed difference in value between the sexes, with images of man above and woman below, was experienced as a damaging source of DISCOURAGEMENT. Girls and women responded with a claim to equal dignity AS IF to say, "Treat me like a man!" Boys and men, feeling in danger of a loss of dignity if they were to appear in any way other than SUPERIOR, pressed a similar claim, AS IF to say. "Treat me like a *real* man!" (Much of this was UNCONSCIOUSLY veiled by the "hysterical" symptoms female patients were presenting to male physicians, such as headaches, fainting spells, and vaginismus; and by the avoidance of women implied in fetishism and SEXUAL phobias that male patients were presenting.) Each was *protesting* that he or she had a right to the kind of dignity that until now was associated with SUPERIORITY.

Relationships between men and women were being disturbed, both outwardly, in the so-called "battle of the sexes," and inwardly by FEELINGS of uneasiness, insecurity, and doubt about the meaning of one's sex to one's value. Freud objected to including a study of these things in psychology. He was convinced, as he put it, that "Anatomy is destiny," and in answer to the term **masculine protest**, constructed the idea of a "penis envy" he took as inherent in what he believed was the attenuated humanity of female sexuality. He also posited a male "castration anxiety" he thought must be an inherited trait from an archaic period of human development. Freud and his supporters were struggling to protect an organismic "libido" theory. To them the **masculine protest** represented too great a departure from physical determinism, thereby threatening the hope of psychology's congruence with the reductionism that characterized the science of that time.

Formal disputations on the **masculine protest** began in the meetings of the Vienna Psychoanalytic Society in 1911, becoming more acrimonious and divisive until Adler resigned his presidency and, with his supporters formed what came to be known as the INDIVIDUAL PSYCHOLOGY Society. As Adler moved further to develop his theory of the INFERIORITY FEELING, and its COMPENSATORY FICTIONAL GOALS, he used the term **masculine protest** less and less, but still regarded it as an important example of the more general striving toward perfection. [See INDIVIDUAL PSYCHOLOGY/ADLERIAN PSYCHOLOGY.]

> The NEUROTIC GOAL of SUPERIORITY is always more or less identified with the masculine role owing to the privileges, both real and imaginary, with which our present culture has invested the male. A girl's FEELING OF INFERIORITY may be markedly increased when she realizes that she is a female, and a boy's also when he doubts his maleness. Both COMPENSATE by an exaggeration of what they imagine to be masculine behavior. This form of COMPENSATION I have called the **masculine protest** (p. 313).

> The NEUROTIC purpose is the enhancement of the SELF-ESTEEM, for which the simplest formula can be recognized in the exaggerated "**masculine protest**." This formula, "I want to be a real man," is the GUIDING FICTION (p. 108).

> In the [PRIVATE] SENSE of the patient, but not in the general [COMMON] SENSE, memories, impulses, and actions are always ARRANGED according to a classification of *INFERIOR=below=feminine* versus *powerful=above=masculine* (p. 249).

MENTAL ILLNESS: ADLER'S UNITARY (UNIFIED) THEORY

Adler framed what has been characterized as a **unitary theory of mental illness** (Adler, 1964). He understood dysfunction, from NEUROSIS to SOCIOPATHY to PSYCHOSIS, as arising from faulty TRAINING AND SELF-TRAINING in childhood, resulting in the child's erroneous evaluations of self, others, and the world, and consequent mistaken MOVEMENT (thought, FEELING, and action), asserting that "All mistaken answers [to the tasks of life] are degrees of an infinite series of failures or ABNORMALITIES, or of the attempts of more or less DISCOURAGED people to solve their life-problems without the use of COOPERATION or SOCIAL INTEREST" (p. 299).

Adler specifies that "certain dynamic forces of the NEUROSES and PSYCHOSES" are present in each case, but that there "are no pure cases"; there are only mixed cases in which, at one time or another, "an aspect of the whole psychic process comes to the foreground." He posited that all cases of misfittedness express "(1) the INFERIORITY FEELING of the child; (2) the SAFEGUARDING tendency and STRIVING for COMPENSATION; (3) a FICTIONAL GOAL of superiority, erected in childhood and thereafter functioning in a TELEOLOGICAL fashion; (4) resulting tested methods, character traits, affects, symptoms, and attitudes in answer to the demands of social interrelatedness; (5) all of these utilized as the means for FICTIONAL self-enhancement in relation to the environment; (6) the seeking of detours and DISTANCE from the expectations of the community in order to escape a real evaluation and personal liability and responsibility; (7) the NEUROTIC perspective and biased devaluation of reality, which may go as far as madness; (8) the elimination of almost all possibilities of human relations and COOPERATION" (p. 300).

Sperry and Carlson (1993) and their contributors, in clear presentations of current thinking in psychology and medicine, discuss the ways in which Adler's **unified theory** relates and does not relate to contemporary approaches to UNDERSTANDING **mental illness,** and provide thoroughgoing expositions of how ADLERIAN PSYCHOLOGY can be utilized and integrated with the categories of psychopathology defined in the *Diagnostic and Statistical Manual of Mental Disorders* (1987, 3rd Rev. ed., known as DSM-3-R), of the American Psychiatric Association. [See ADLERIAN PSYCHOTHERAPY.]

> The NEUROSIS and PSYCHOSIS are attempts at COMPENSATION, creations of the psyche which result from the accentuated and exaggerated guiding idea of the child who has an accentuated INFERIORITY FEELING. The insecurity of these children regarding their future and success in life compels them toward stronger efforts and SAFEGUARDS in their FICTIONAL life plan [LIFESTYLE] and toward detours around the problems of life. The more fixed and rigid their guiding image [GUIDING FICTION], the more dogmatically will they draw the GUIDING LINES of their life (p. 282).

MISTAKEN GOALS OF THE DISCOURAGED CHILD

Adler considered each individual AS IF he or she were in MOVEMENT from an intolerable feeling of MINUS toward a desired feeling of PLUS, with a personally-created GOAL of success CONCRETIZED in an image of status or condition that would conquer the INFERIORITY FEELING. Dreikurs saw that among children these GOALS could be seen as reflecting the desire to have a distinctive and recognized place of BELONGING amongst others. He also saw that **discouraged children**, who regard themselves as unable to accomplish such a GOAL on the socially USEFUL SIDE of life, through COOPERATION and CONTRIBUTION, do not surrender the struggle, but are more likely than the others to develop erroneous images of success, and to choose **mistaken goals** in pursuit of such images.

Dreikurs (1964) posited four such **mistaken goals of the discouraged child** in a schema which has proven to be of immense help to teachers, counselors, and others concerned with the EDUCATION and welfare of children and their development. These **mistaken goals** are (a) *attention* (annoying or disruptive behavior that says, "I may not be much, but I will not be ignored."); (b) *power* (angry, insistent, often in progression from the efforts of others to stop the attention-getting antics); (c) *revenge* (bitter, hurtful words and actions, often in response to the harsh punishments of retaliatory *power*, and expressing the unhappy conviction of a child who believes he is not loved or is not lovable); (d) the *display of inadequacy* (reflecting a despair of doing anything that will be successful or appreciated). Dreikurs also systematized techniques for recognizing a child's **mistaken goal**, precise methods for disclosing the **mistaken goal** to the child without punishing or shaming, opening the eyes of PARENTS to recognize the meaning and desire for significance in the **mistaken goals** of misbehavior, and ENCOURAGING children to consider openings to useful participation and CONTRIBUTION. [See ADOLESCENCE.]

See Grunwald, B. B. & McAbee, H. V. (1999); Walton, F. X. & Powers, R. L. (1974).

MOST MEMORABLE OBSERVATION

The **Most Memorable Observation (MMO)** is a technique introduced by Francis X. Walton that employs an individual's pre-teen and teen memories to uncover a person's beliefs as these relate to *parenting styles.*

The **MMO** has proven particularly useful when parents find it difficult to adopt more effective skills because their goal of helping the child is compromised by their guarding against falling into positions of inferiority. The **MMO** helps the therapist identify the negative behavior they may be guarding against that prevents their becoming more successful parents.

Its use is not only applicable in parent consultation. The mistaken thinking revealed in the **most memorable observation** also helps clients address problems in personal and professional relationships, helps teachers see how mistaken beliefs influence their use of problematic methods of leadership and discipline, helps therapists and clients in LIFESTYLE formulation, and has been adapted for use in couple counseling.

To obtain the **most memorable observation** the therapist asks the following question:

> Sometimes in our early teenage years, or even in late preteen years, it seems very common for each of us to look around our family life and draw a conclusion about some aspect of life that appears to be important. Sometimes it is positive, "I really like this aspect of life in our family." Often it is negative, "I don't like this at all. This is really distasteful. When I get to be an adult, I am going to do everything I can to keep this from occurring in my family." What was it for you? As you think of life in your family at about age 11, 12, 13 or so, what conclusion do you think you drew? It may have been positive, it may have been negative, or it may have been both. [See PARENTING.]

See Walton, F. X. (1990; 1996).

MOVEMENT/LAW OF MOVEMENT

Movement is Adler's term for what other theorists call behavior (which is not to say that Adler never used the latter term, as the next to last of the quotations, below, illustrates). **Movement** is meant to include all thought, FEELING, and physical activity; the **law of movement** of the individual is therefore the basis of the STYLE OF LIVING. **Movement** connotes the UNDERSTANDING of human being as always in process,[6] moving away from the FELT MINUS toward a subjectively-conceived FICTIONAL PLUS position, away from the intolerable feelings of worthlessness (G., *Minderwertigkeit*) toward the desired feelings of mastery and worthwhileness (G., *Vollwertigkeit*). [See CONCRETIZATION OF THE GOAL; INFERIORITY FEELING; SUPERIORITY STRIVING]

> Human life . . . expresses itself in **movement** and direction toward [successful solutions] (p. 163).

> The **law of movement** in the mental life of a person is the decisive factor for his individuality (p. 195).

> All is **movement** (p. 195).

> It is necessary to freeze the **movement** to see it as form (p. 195).

> The findings of INDIVIDUAL PSYCHOLOGY point to the fact that all the behavior [**movement**] of a human being fits into a unit and is an expression of the individual's STYLE OF LIFE (p. 358).

> Where there is tension there is action in the central nervous system; the individual drums on the table, plucks at his lip or tears up pieces of paper; he has to MOVE in some way. . . . By means of the autonomic nervous system, the tension is communicated to the whole body (p. 224).

NATURAL OR LOGICAL CONSEQUENCES

Dreikurs and Grey (1968) published a system for TRAINING the child in an atmosphere of mutual respect through the use of **natural or logical consequences**. Although the idea was an old one, as the citation from Robert G. Ingersoll (1833-1899), below, indicates, their system represents a practical method parents may employ that enables children to experience both the satisfying and unpleasant **consequences** of their choices and actions. This does away with the forms of parental GUIDANCE and direction that entail lecturing, nagging, punishing, and other instruments of DISCOURAGEMENT. Dreikurs and Grey recognized that the emerging democratic family required new tools to replace the praise/reward and shame/punishment methods which characterize the fading autocratic tradition. **Natural consequences** follow upon the child's behavior without PARENTAL intervention. PARENTS are taught to allow their children to experience the outcomes of their own actions. *Logical* **consequences**, however, must be discussed and agreed upon among the affected family members in advance of their applications, preferably in the CONTEXT of the regular FAMILY MEETING. If not agreed upon in advance and in this consensus-finding forum, the **consequences** are more likely to be experienced as punishments from above to below than as outcomes of personal choice and actions. The use of **natural or logical consequences** enhances the child's developing sense of him- or herself as a responsible participant in shaping the character of family life, as well as the circumstances of his or her own individual life. Anything can be abused in practice, and it must be noted that "**consequences**" invoked during a power struggle are experienced by children as punishment. A power struggle should be taken as the sign of a general breakdown of COOPERATION, and its **natural consequence** is the requirement to start over, and to discover what is required on all sides to make peace.

In nature there are neither rewards nor punishments. There are only **consequences** (Ingersoll, ¶ 5).

71

NEUROSIS: "YES, BUT . . ."

Adler's phrase, "**Yes, but** . . ." was his shorthand description of **neurotic** operations. The **neurotic** recognizes the requirements of living ("**Yes**, I see what is required of me . . ."); however, he or she seeks an exemption through excuses, alibis, HESITATION, or other maneuvers ("**but** I can't do it because . . . ."). Here the person puts forth his or her reasons, and there are as many such "reasons" as there are avoiding and HESITATING human beings. The "**Yes — but**" is linked to the sense of DISCOURAGEMENT which these individuals feel in the face of life's challenges, and is an expression of the HESITATING ATTITUDE.

> Every **neurotic** professes the best of intentions. He is quite convinced of the necessity for SOCIAL INTEREST and for meeting the problems of life. Only in his case there is an exception to this universal demand (p. 303).

> **Neurosis** is always behavior which can be expressed in two words, the words "**yes — but**" (p. 302).

> In every case there is a "**yes**" that emphasizes the pressure of SOCIAL INTEREST, but this is invariably followed by a "**but**" that possesses greater strength and prevents the necessary increase of SOCIAL INTEREST (p. 157).

> By "yes" I mean that the **neurotic** person recognizes COMMON SENSE [an expression of SOCIAL INTEREST]. He sees that there is a particular problem before him and he says **yes**, but he does not follow it up. It is always followed by "**but**" (p. 302).

> Every **neurotic** symptom is designed to provide a justification for a refusal to solve the problems of life, without lowering the sense of personal SUPERIORITY (Adler, 1980, p. 186).

> I must win [the patient] . . . and take her part as far as possible.
> Every **neurotic** is partly right (p. 334).

NORMAL vs. ABNORMAL

Adler named his task to be the understanding of individual UNIQUENESS, and Adlerians have therefore generally eschewed the terms **normal** and **abnormal** as not USEFUL for this purpose. As terms pertinent to statistical measures, they are of little if any value to the examination and discussion of the INDIVIDUAL VARIANT. Instead Adlerians use as a standard (for what others call **normal** or **abnormal**) the extent of COMMUNITY FEELING/SOCIAL INTEREST expressed in a person's MOVEMENT (thought, FEELING, and action).

> The degree of a person's SOCIAL INTEREST determines his ability and willingness to function socially. . . . Adler found that SOCIAL INTEREST was the gauge for defining **normalcy**, both for the individual and for the group (Dreikurs, 1971, p. ix).

> SOCIAL INTEREST is the barometer of the child's **normality** (p. 154).

> [From the sociological point of view] the **normal** man is an individual who lives in society and whose mode of life is so adapted that, whether he wants it or not, society derives a certain advantage from his work. From the psychological point of view, he has enough energy and COURAGE to meet the problems and difficulties as they come along. Both of these qualities are missing in the case of **abnormal** persons. They are neither socially adjusted nor are they psychologically adjusted to the daily TASKS OF LIFE (p. 154).

> Adler draws no line of distinction between **normal** and **abnormal** people: for him the former make the smaller, the latter the bigger mistakes (Orgler, 1963, p. 107).

OPEN FORUM FAMILY COUNSELING/COMMUNITY CHILD GUIDANCE CENTERS

Adler introduced the practice of counseling in an open setting in 1922 in Vienna, at a time when a progressive government was supportive of experimentation in EDUCATION. By 1934, when the Fascists came to power in Austria, there were 32 **Child Guidance Centers** in the schools and community centers of Vienna. Attendance at **child guidance** programs was open to all persons interested in the EDUCATION of children: parents, teachers, social workers, school principals, and others. Adler and those he trained met with a child and his or her teacher (or a child and his or her PARENTS) and counseled them in front of the others present. At the conclusion of the session, those present were invited to talk about what they had learned and to ask questions about their own situations. Adler conducted **public child guidance** sessions on lecture tours in the United States, and continued doing so after immigrating to the United States and taking up residence in New York City. Adler's method was carried forward by Dreikurs, who opened the first **Community Child Guidance Center** in Chicago in 1939. In a variety of applications Adler's method has been continued by counselors trained by Dreikurs and by Dreikurs's students.

> [Following the techniques developed by Dr. Alfred Adler], GROUP THERAPY in . . . [**Community Child Guidance Centers** of Chicago] is a unique combination of group dynamics . . . taking place at many levels: the family group, in which we deal with the entire family in each case rather than with the mother and child alone; the children's group, in the game room, where we supplement play with psychodrama as a further GROUP approach; the parents' group, composed of parents enrolled for therapy, who participate in group discussions; the community group, composed of visiting parents, teachers, students, and others interested in problems of **child guidance**, who likewise participate in the discussion; [and] children among the adults, being interviewed in the counseling room in the presence of adults — one of the most interesting, and perhaps most controversial, aspects of our GROUP THERAPY (Dreikurs, 1974, p. 86).

For a description of contemporary **open forum family counseling**, see Christensen, O. C. & Marchant, W. C. (2004), "The Family Counseling Process," pp. 29-58; for guidelines on establishing a center, see Grunwald, B. B. & McAbee, H. V. (1999), "The Family Counseling Center," pp. 311-315; for a thorough-going account of Adler's Vienna **child guidance clinics**, see Ganz, M. (1953), "The Medico-Pedagogic Councils," pp. 109-175; for an historical account of Dreikurs's part in bringing Adlerian psychology and Adler's practice of **open forum counseling** to America in the face of a hostile psychiatric and psychoanalytic establishment's opposition, see Terner, J. & Pew, W. L. (1978).

ORGAN DIALECT/ORGAN JARGON/ORGAN LANGUAGE

Adler used the terms **organ dialect, organ jargon,** and **organ language** interchangeably to refer to somatic signs and symptoms that express (though veiled) an individual's attitudes and opinions. The Adler Bibliography compiled by H. L. and R. R. Ansbacher (pp. 465-470) shows that Adler used the term **organ dialect** as early as 1912, when he wrote a paper of that name. He later borrowed the term **organ jargon** that had been coined by Georg Groddeck (cited in Robb, 1932), and also synonymously employed the term **organ language**. **Organ dialect**, like other MOVEMENT of the person, is understood as purposive, that is, whether or not CONSCIOUSLY, in line with the individual's unique LAW OF MOVEMENT. The **jargon** or statement made by the organ is UNIQUE, and its selection is idiosyncratic, consistent with the individual's particular ORGAN INFERIORITY or the organ's availability as already rehearsed for symptomatic expression, or according to any symbolic meaning the individual has attached to the selected organ. For example, two persons may suffer from leg pains that have no basis in organic disease. The **jargon** of one may be: "I can't stand on my own two feet," expressing a conviction that he or she must depend on the help of others to meet life's challenges, while the **jargon** of the other may be: "I can't stand it!" declaring an inability to endure a particular pressure or difficult situation. As to the symbolic aspect of the symptom, one might discover that a client, experiencing heart trouble for which there is no medical explanation, is expressing heartbreak. [See ORGAN INFERIORITY.]

> The body is also subject to the LAW OF MOVEMENT (p. 223).

> [The functions of the body] speak a language which is usually more expressive and discloses the individual's opinion more clearly than words are able to do. Still it is a language, the language of the body, which I have called **organ dialect** (p. 223).

> Each individual's body speaks in a language of its own (p. 225).

> An organ can never "speak its **dialect**" unless the individual permits it to "speak" — unless he has a use for this symptom in his life-plan [LIFESTYLE] in the pursuit of his fictive LIFE-GOAL (Dreikurs, R., 1973, p. 144).

> Some day it will probably be proved that every ORGAN INFERIORITY may respond to psychological influences and speak the **organ language**, that is, a language expressing the attitude of the individual toward the problems confronting him (p. 308).

> It is always necessary to look for . . . reciprocal actions of the mind on the body, and of the body on the mind, for both of them are parts of the whole with which we are concerned (p. 225).

> Sometimes the mouth lies or the head does not understand; but the functions of the body always speak the truth (p. 434).

See Griffith, J. (1984).

ORGAN INFERIORITY

In Adlerian Psychology, **organ inferiorities** are discussed in two domains. First, in Adler's original UNDERSTANDING of **organ inferiorities** as the underlying motive for human forward MOVEMENT, and second, in relation to the TRAINING AND SELF-TRAINING of children who are OVERBURDENED with **organ inferiorities.**

As regards the first domain: Adler, as a physician, noticed that human beings STRIVE to OVERCOME their **organ inferiorities** by means of *physical* COMPENSATIONS, and he proposed **organ inferiorities** as the basis for human STRIVING. In his first medical book (1907/1917), *Study of Organ Inferiority and its Psychical Compensations*, he presents the idea of COMPENSATION and its tendency toward OVER-COMPENSATION. At the time of writing, Adler's concerns were directed toward the limited field of objective observations and diagnoses; INFERIORITY FEELINGS or other subjective materials were not in his purview. In his later work, however, he came to see that COMPENSATION and OVER-COMPENSATION operate both physically *and* psychologically.

Seeking a more encompassing explanation for human motivation, Adler next proposed the concept of the MASCULINE PROTEST. In this new turn, Adler took into account human beings' subjective assessments of their situations in life. Freud's view of the female as a deformed male consumed with envy for the penis was devised in reaction to Adler's thinking, and was complicit in confirming a belief in female INFERIORITY generally held at that time (and into this time). Observing a society in which boys and men had unassailable positions of dominance, and in which girls and women were invariably disrespected and subordinated, Adler posited that the demand females might make, if they were able to verbalize their feelings, would be "Treat me like a man!", and that those boys and men with exaggerated ideas of masculine power (and a matching apprehension of falling short of it) might also press to be treated like "a *real* man!"

Adler reached his conclusive understanding of the origins of human STRIVING when he came to see that both **organ inferiorities** and the MASCULINE PROTEST were *particular forms* of a more general and *universal* INFERIORITY FEELING that is, in itself, the spur to STRIVING.

The second domain of **organ inferiorities** in Adler's work addresses child development. Adler noted that some children endure unusually stressful, OVERBURDENING CHILDHOOD SITUATIONS, and that among these (along with pampered and neglected, abused, unwanted, and hated children) is the situation of the child with **organ inferiorities.** [See COMPENSATION/OVER-COMPENSATION; MASCULINE PROTEST; OVERBURDENING CHILDHOOD SITUATIONS.]

> We understand that children with **inferior organs** will feel inadequate for the TASKS OF LIFE and that the MINUS situation will be felt by a child with **inferior organs** more intensely than by the average child. . . . The organic weakness does not *necessarily* function as a MINUS situation, but the child *experiences* the weakness of his organic equipment for average social tasks, and he feels impelled to reorganize it accordingly (Adler, 1979, p. 88).

> The INFERIORITY FEELING constantly presses toward its own resolution (Adler, 1979, p. 58).

OVERBURDENING CHILDHOOD SITUATIONS

Adler identified three childhood situations as **overburdening**, all characterized by abnormal stresses placed upon children in particularly difficult circumstances. There are (a) children who experience severe ORGAN INFERIORITIES; (b) children who are pampered; (c) children who suffer from neglect, abuse, or from being hated and unwanted. In situations such as these, where children are not welcomed, are not ENCOURAGED, cannot see PLACES of value open to them, and are unable to believe in what they can do on the socially USEFUL SIDE of life, the probabilities for the development of COURAGE and COOPERATION are gravely diminished, and the likelihood of the development of dysfunctional STYLES OF LIVING is markedly increased. [See SEXUALITY.]

> Children born with INFERIOR ORGANS experience their bodies and its pains and weaknesses as a burden. They, much more than normal children, develop INFERIORITY FEELINGS, strive to COMPENSATE these lacks and to arrive at a GOAL in which they foresee and presume a feeling of SUPERIORITY. In this MOVEMENT . . . they are attacked much more by the difficulties of life and feel and live as though they were in an enemy country. Fighting, hesitating, stopping, escaping . . . they are . . . lacking in SOCIAL INTEREST, COURAGE, and self-confidence because they fear defeat more than they desire success (p. 118).

> We find this great FEELING OF INFERIORITY also among PAMPERED children. Living in a kind of symbiosis, like parasites, always connected with their mother, their GOAL OF SUPERIORITY is to make this relationship permanent. Each change terrifies them. . . . Later in life they are not adapted for occupation, love, and marriage, because they consider their own welfare and are not looking for the interests of others. . . . [They are] the majority of the problem children. . . . [Abused, neglected, hated, and unwanted children] feel curtailed and behave like enemies. . . . Their GOAL OF SUPERIORITY is to suppress the other person. . . . They are lacking in SOCIAL INTEREST and therefore in COURAGE and self-confidence (pp. 118-119).

> [The pampered child] is granted prominence without working to deserve it and will generally come to feel this prominence as a birthright (p. 369).

> We know that every pampered child becomes a hated child. . . . Neither society nor the family wishes to continue the pampering indefinitely (Adler, 1969, p. 10).

> All great accomplishments stem from the blessed struggle with the needs of childhood — be they organ inferiorities, pampering, or oppressing circumstances — as long as the child, at the time of his oppression, has already learned the active ADAPTATION to COOPERATION. Then, and also later on, in the face of all difficulties and torments, only the paths to COOPERATION will be open in accordance with his inviolable LAW OF MOVEMENT (Adler, 1979, p. 54).

See Adler, 1956, pp. 417-420.

PARADOX/ANTI-SUGGESTION

Dreikurs saw these terms as descriptive of Adler's catching the imagination of the client and redirecting his or her attention from the USELESS to the USEFUL SIDE. Regarding a particular symptom, against which the client has been fighting a losing battle, Adler asked (for example, about a nervous tic), "How bad does it get? Can you show me how it looks when it is worse than it is now?" Suddenly the field shifts. The heroism of resistance is put aside for a deliberate performance of the symptom for clinical examination. The power of the symptom until now has been its involuntary "possession" of the person, and his or her valiant but unsuccessful struggle against it. Now the client finds he is unable to proceed. He is embarrassed. His conscience holds him in check, and he feels as if "caught out" by his own awareness of his responsibility.

As remarkable as it was then for Adler's students first witnessing the technique, **paradox** is commonplace in counseling today. A. Maslow, R. May, and C. Rogers, recognized as "the major theorists . . . to have prepared the ground for Humanistic Psychology" (Aanstoos, C, Serlin, I., & Greening, T., 2000, Contents section 1, ¶4), all studied with Adler (Ansbacher, 1990): it is fair to assume that they passed on his interventions, which are now part of everyday practice for counselors in the United States and elsewhere.

According to Mozdzierz, G. J., Macchitelli, F. J., and Lisiecki, J. (1976, p. 169), while **paradox** (also called **anti-suggestion**) is part of Zen tradition, Adler was the innovator of its use in psychiatry in the West. The purpose of **paradox** is to purge the symptom, either by encouraging the client to practice it, or by predicting its eruption. By performing the symptom, the client demonstrates control over it; by predicting the emergence of the symptom, the therapist challenges the client to exhibit the symptom as predicted and so to confirm the therapist's skill, which the client is reluctant to do. (See DEPRECIATION TENDENCY.) An example is Adler's telling an anxious patient, who was gulping air when feeling conflicted, to "swallow some air quickly" at those times. Adler reported that, after this advice, the client "began to control himself, and discontinued the habit" (Adler, 1964b, p. 346). Wexberg (1970), using the term "negationary tactics," tells of a patient who reports that, after a long period of dependency, he is going to go back to work. Wexberg says the therapist may respond with skepticism, saying that returning to work is only an intention, and besides, "It is too soon . . . [you] must not be too hasty" (pp. 90-91). B. H. Shulman, in a footnote to this case (p. 92), states "When the therapist 'suggests' to the patient that perhaps he should remain dependent and continue to avoid responsibility, it often becomes a matter of pride to the patient to prove that he *can* be independent and responsible. Thus, if the patient improves, it becomes the patient's triumph, not the therapist's. This tactic uses the patient's own oppositional tendencies . . . to induce the patient to 'put down' the therapist [DEPRECIATION TENDENCY] by changing his relation to life for the better." Carich (1997) states "**Paradoxical** interventions are based upon 'AS IF' philosophy and future orientation." In **paradoxical intention**, "the client is told to behave 'AS IF' he has the symptoms." In **paradoxical prediction**, therapists disrupt a pattern by predicting the recurrence of the symptom. In both cases, "The goal is to allow the client to experience the problem in a different context" (p. 157).

In counseling a schoolgirl who makes trouble at school, Adler suggested saying, " 'School is the most important thing in the world, and if I were you I would make even a greater fuss about it.' By this *reductio ad absurdum* I would spoil her pleasure in her tactics" (p. 398). [See SPITTING IN THE SOUP.]

> If one succeeds in persuading a patient to produce the symptoms deliberately, they will disappear (Dreikurs, 1973, p. 129).

> [A technique] which not only yields results with amazing promptness but affords theoretical insight into the mechanism of the "nervous" symptoms was described repeatedly by Alfred Adler and has been called by Erwin Wexberg "**anti-suggestion**" . . . . The patient is advised . . . to practice the very thing which up to now he has apparently been fighting against . . . . One can observe again and again . . . that the symptom diminishes in intensity when the patient consciously tries to intensify it . . . . When he ceases to struggle [against the symptom] and the tension abates, the symptom, too, disappears (Dreikurs, 1973, p. 129).

See "Paradox," Sherman, R. & Fredman, N. (1986), pp. 189-228.

PARENTING

"As the child needs training, so do the **parents**" (Dreikurs, 1964, p. viii).

Dreikurs conducted OPEN FORUM PUBLIC FAMILY COUNSELING to help **parents** and children (who volunteered to work with him in the public setting) understand, address, and resolve their difficulties. Simultaneously, he taught his method and approach to those who observed the sessions: other **parents**, counselors and therapists, teachers, and other professionals.

Since Dreikurs's innovation, beginning in 1938, based on the child guidance work of Alfred Adler in New York City and Vienna (which Dreikurs had been privileged to observe), a host of materials on **parenting** (books, classes, trainings, seminars, workshops, video and electronic opportunities by numerous authors) have become available and eagerly used by **parents** everywhere. Why is this necessary? Why is it that for the first time in history (as Dreikurs provocatively asked) a living creature has appeared on the planet that doesn't know how to raise its own young?

Adler and Dreikurs became aware that the old order, which broadly supported promises, rewards, and praise (on the one hand), and threats and punishment (on the other hand) for the TRAINING of children, was breaking down. In its place the evolving culture of freedom and EQUALITY was shaping the world of the young. **Parents,** at a loss, needed an approach suitable to the new order. Dreikurs, applying the basic principles of ADLERIAN PSYCHOLOGY, emphasized respect for the dignity of the child. Instead of rewards, he stressed taking pleasure in what the child accomplishes *for the child's sake* rather than for **parental** aggrandizement: "You must have enjoyed getting that 'A.' " Instead of praise, he stressed ENCOURAGEMENT: "The important thing is the effort you put into the project." Instead of punishment, he stressed the importance of FAMILY COUNCIL (FAMILY MEETING) for solving family problems and the use of natural or agreed-upon logical consequences in TRAINING children in responsibility. [See ADOLESCENCE; MISTAKEN GOALS OF THE DISCOURAGED CHILD; SIBLING RIVALRY (COMPETITION); MOST MEMORABLE OBSERVATION.]

See Dreikurs, R. (1964); Dinkmeyer, D. C, Jr., & McKay, G. D. (1998); Grunwald, B. B., & McAbee, H. V. (1999); McKay, G. D., & Maybell, S. A. (2004); Nelsen, J. (1996); Platt, J. M. (1989); Popkin, M. (1993); Walton, F. X., & Powers, R. L. (1974); Walton, F. X. (1990; 1996).

PHENOMENOLOGY

This may be defined as a study of the apprehension of the self and the external world according to the way these things appear to an individual in his or her unique, subjective evaluation. The term is from the Greek, *phainomenon*, meaning appearance. INDIVIDUAL PSYCHOLOGY pursues a **phenomenological** UNDERSTANDING of the person's unique LIFE-STYLE, seen as the expression of a private and CREATIVE assessment of self and the world.

> We do not suffer from the shock of our experiences — the so-called trauma — but we make out of them just what suits our purposes. . . . Meanings are not determined by situations, but we determine ourselves by the meanings we give to situations (p. 208).

> I am convinced that a person's behavior springs from his opinion. We should not be surprised at this, because our senses do not receive actual facts, but merely a subjective image of them, a reflection of the external world. *Omnia ad opinionem suspensa sunt.* [Everything depends upon opinion. — Seneca] (p. 182).

> [The individual] relates himself [to the outside world] always according to his own interpretation of himself and of his present problem (p. 206).

> We are influenced not by facts but by our opinion of facts (p. 192).

> Perception is more than a simple physical phenomenon; it is a psychic function from which we may draw the most far going conclusions concerning the inner life (Adler, 1957, p. 50).

PRIVATE LOGIC/ PRIVATE MEANING/ PRIVATE SENSE vs. COMMON SENSE

Private logic, a term R. Dreikurs and H. L. Ansbacher each adapted from Adler's "private intelligence" (Adler, 1969, p. 72), describes the FICTIONAL line of reasoning proceeding from **private meaning,** that is, meaning premised upon the person's private and unique valuation of self, others, and the world, and what life requires of him or her. **Private logic,** AS IF reasoning that dysfunctional, erratic, and anti-social behavior is necessary, is the fiction of a hidden argument. **Private sense** in a pattern of conviction is not CONSCIOUS. It is an artifact of the psychotherapeutic transaction, revealed by indirection, AS IF particular thoughts and ideas were operating to require self-defeating or otherwise damaging behavior.

In Adlerian therapy an individual's behavior (thought, FEELING, and action) is explained to the client AS IF it were a conclusion required by a **private logic,** as client and therapist uncover the **private meaning** which the client has relied upon for answering such questions as: (a) What kind of a person am I? (b) What kind of a world is this? (c) What must I, as a person such as I am, do in a world such as this is in order to MAKE A PLACE for myself? In sum, the effort to CLARIFY the **private meaning** asks, "What would have to be true to make an otherwise particular, peculiar, and socially senseless pattern of behavior, intelligible?" The INDIVIDUAL PSYCHOLOGIST thus assumes that the person is acting AS IF the behavior were an intelligent response in the situation, according to a **private logic,** answering the requirements of a **private meaning.**

Common sense is that UNDERSTANDING and evaluation of life which can be held in common with the broader community. In the PSYCHOCLARITY process (Powers and Griffith, 1987), reconsideration of the usefulness of the **private meaning** for successful adaptation arises in an examination of the extent of the congruence of a **private sense** with the **common sense.** By making the **private logic** of the client explicit, client and therapist subject it to the awareness of its leading to a departure from our **common sense,** shared by counselee and counselor, in deference to which each is subject to correction, and neither corrects the other. Both now meet in acknowledging this **common sense** as the reality that alone serves as a correction to any ERRORS.

> There are some people who . . . give a **private meaning** to life. . . . We find . . . that such people are unable to connect themselves with their fellow man (p. 253).

> The meaning [all failures] give to life is a **private meaning.** . . . A **private meaning** is, in fact, no meaning at all. Meaning is only possible in communication (p. 156).

> A **private meaning** can never be put to the test. The mark of all true "meanings of life" is that they are common meanings, that is, meanings in which others can share and which others can accept as valid. . . . UNDERSTANDING is a common matter, not a private function (p. 253).

> We must distinguish between "private intelligence" and "**common sense,**" and must understand reason as being connected with **common sense** — sense that can be shared (p. 253).

> By reason we understand, with Kant, a process which has general validity. Hence, by reasonable we understand **common sense.** We may define **common sense** as all those forms of expression and as the content of all behavior which we find beneficial to the community (p. 149).

> Reason is inseparably connected with SOCIAL INTEREST (p. 149).

> If the patient can abandon his dream . . . born of his vanity . . . [he will] begin to feel himself an EQUAL among EQUALS. . . . His COURAGE, too will mount and his reason and "**common sense**" will increase and gain control where heretofore he has been under the sway of his "**private sense**" (p. 333).

81

PROFESSIONAL RESPONSIBILITY

Adler took the ethical high ground in his opinions about **professional responsibility** toward clients and the common life. As a proponent of Marxist-Socialist concepts, he was a supporter of causes for social betterment, from health issues to government regulation of working conditions to FEMINISM. His first publication at age 28 was *Health Book for the Tailoring Trade* (1898), an attack on the conditions in which tailors worked, in which he described the connection between "the economic condition of a trade and its disease," and argued *for* government protection and *against* unrestrained capitalism (Hoffman, 1994, pp. 35-37). His further writings tell us that in professional work it is essential to convey attitudes of respect, EQUALITY, COOPERATION, and concern toward clients, and that in the public sphere it is essential to participate in promoting COMMUNITY FEELING, supporting social justice, and ameliorating the effects of disconnectedness and hostility.

> The honest psychologist cannot shut his eyes to social conditions which prevent the child from becoming a part of the community and from feeling at home in the world, and which allow him to grow up as though he lived in enemy country. Thus the psychologist must work against nationalism when it is so poorly understood that it harms mankind as a whole; against wars of conquest, revenge, and prestige; against unemployment which plunges people into hopelessness; and against all other obstacles which interfere with the spreading of SOCIAL INTEREST in the family, the school, and society at large (p. 454).

> The problem of human nature is one which presents an enormous task, whose solution has been the GOAL of our culture since time immemorial. It is a science that cannot be pursued with the sole purpose of developing occasional experts. Only the UNDERSTANDING of human nature by every human being can be its proper GOAL (Adler, 1957, p. 15).

> INDIVIDUAL PSYCHOLOGY aims at serving the community rather than forging new arms for a caste of scholars. . . . It must hand over all its knowledge and skills to the community. . . . It will never do to permit less knowledge to the teacher, the PARENTS, the patient, than to the physician (Adler, 1978, p. 253-254).

PSYCHOCLARITY/UNDERSTANDING

Psychoclarity is a neologism introduced by Powers and Griffith (1982) to improve **understanding** of the processes involved in psychotherapy.[5] In his writings on psychiatric counseling Adler distinguishes the INDIVIDUAL PSYCHOLOGY method from any practice that assumes diseased or deficient constitutions. He focuses instead on ERRORS made in early childhood before acquisition of discriminating language, and so not subject to rational challenge. Such ERRORS are maintained, as if needed to SAFEGUARD a DISCOURAGED person from humiliation and defeat. Chief among these ideas is that of individual life as a solitary, SELF-BOUNDED project, the success of which requires a COMPETITIVE struggle against others. The corrective to this ERROR is an **understanding** of the community of human life, and ultimately of the cosmos itself, as the reality in which each plays a part, and the further development of which is the common task in which all personal value is to be found. This is the COMMUNITY FEELING/SOCIAL INTEREST, never completely extinguished by any PRIVATE MEANING, and always in need of cultivation, that is, of GUIDANCE and EDUCATION that is the legacy of culture. It is the task of the counselor to **clarify** and further this **understanding**, and so to stimulate the growth of COMMUNITY FEELING, the true COMPENSATION for all personal feelings of INFERIORITY.

Using the image of "mind" as the repository of **understanding** (and of misunderstanding) Powers and Griffith (1982) described the **psychoclarity** formula as: "You cannot change your mind until you know your mind; you cannot know your mind until you can speak your mind and your speech brings your PRIVATE SENSE into the COMMON SENSE world" (p. 1). This is the therapeutic encounter. The original ERRORS of a child, hitherto *unspeakable*, are put into words, examined, and subjected to correction by the shared COMMON SENSE of client and therapist. "When I know my mind I can see that, while the past behavior was ***understandable,*** it is no longer *necessary.*" [See CONTEXT PSYCHOLOGY VS. DEPTH PSYCHOLOGY.]

> [INDIVIDUAL PSYCHOLOGY theory] undisturbed by any inconsistency . . . is different with the interpretation of the individual forms of expression, their **understanding** within a **clarified** self-consistent CONTEXT, and with treatment. In these respects artistic ability is a prerequisite . . . [to] be attained only through self-knowledge, quick repartee, persuasiveness, conviction, and sufficient ability to GUESS, to identify, and to COOPERATE. Although all these abilities overlap, their development is different in everyone who practices INDIVIDUAL PSYCHOLOGY (Adler, 1979, p. 282).

> This incontrovertible **clarification** of the errors in a LIFE STYLE, certainly no easy task, persuades and produces the new LIFE STYLE, which is actively adapted, not entirely to the existing reality, but to the growing, becoming reality (Adler, 1979, p. 293).

> The stronger emphasis on **understanding** in our form of treatment, on comprehending MISTAKES . . . still generally human, prevents the counselee from becoming frightened (Adler, 1979, p. 300).

> INDIVIDUAL PSYCHOLOGY wants to train fellow men; it must therefore prove its fellowmanship in its dealing with the erring. Only in this spirit can the erring individual be won for COOPERATION; only in this way is it possible to give him a **clear understanding** of his mistaken STYLE OF LIFE. The healing process . . . begins with winning the erring human child for COOPERATION. But the cure [is his] own work . . . after he has gained adequate **understanding** (Adler, 1979, p. 306).

> A real explanation must be so **clear** that the patient knows and feels his own experience instantly (p. 335).

> We are far from denying that other schools of psychiatry have their successes . . . but in our experience they do so less by their methods than when they happen to give the patient a good human relationship with the physician, or above all, to give him ENCOURAGEMENT. . . . The cure of all mental disorder lies in the . . . laborious process of making the patient **understand** his own MISTAKES (p. 343).

83

PSYCHOLOGICAL BIRTH-ORDER POSITION/BIRTH-ORDER VANTAGE

Adler was the first investigator in modern psychology to note the significance of **psychological birth-order position** in the development and dynamics of personality. **Psychological birth-order position** is the **vantage** from which the child perceives and evaluates self, others, and the world, and from which the child forms convictions about what is required of — as well as what is open to — him or her. It is distinguished from ordinal position in consideration of other factors contributing to the child's sense of PLACE in the family, including gender, age differences, death, absence, or incapacity of a sibling. For example, a son born following the birth of a daughter (or daughters) may still be regarded as having a "first-born" position. The same may be true for a daughter born following the birth of a son (or sons). Where there is a large number of siblings the male and female children may enumerate themselves in separate categories as first, second, and third-born (etc.) sons or daughters. [See DETHRONEMENT.] While Adler associated certain characteristics with each *position*, and these provide a framework for GUESSING, they are not to be considered as a way of TYPING the individuals *in* any one of the positions.

Unlike many other students of the individual's development in a family-of-origin, Adler went beyond attention to the importance of **birth order**, GENDER GUIDING LINES, and other matters regularly regarded as *influences upon* the child. He also gave his attention to what is obvious, even though regularly overlooked, namely the *influence of* each child on the shape and character of the FAMILY CONSTELLATION into which it is born.

> It is a common fallacy to imagine that children of the same family are formed in the same ENVIRONMENT. Of course there is much which is the same for all children in the same home, but the psychological situation of each child is individual and differs from that of others, because of the order of their succession (p. 376).

> It is not, of course, the child's number . . . which influences his character, but the *situation* into which he is born and the way in which he interprets it (p. 377).

For a report and discussion of the *White-Campbell Psychological Birth Order Inventory* (1991) and the *Birth Role Repertory Grid* (1994), developed by White, J., Campbell, L., and Stewart A. E., see Oberst, U. E. & Stewart, A. E. (2003), pp. 170-181.

[Most general texts in Adlerian Psychology, especially those on parenting and child guidance, address the birth-order of the children, not all with the same emphases.]

PSYCHOLOGY OF USE vs. PSYCHOLOGY OF POSSESSION

Adler's view was that the unique MOVEMENT and LIFESTYLE of an individual in all thought, FEELING, and action cannot be accounted for as the outcome or consequence of prior conditions, forces, or influences, (i.e., causes), but must be understood in terms of the **use** to which the individual puts these things. In this approach, the psychologist does not seek an UNDERSTANDING of individuals by identifying traits, which they are supposed to **possess** (for example, laziness, bad temper), but rather in observing the ways they make **use** of their various capacities and opportunities in line with their GOALS.

> The direction and the directed utilization of instincts and drives, as well as impressions from the ENVIRONMENT and EDUCATION, are the artistic work of the child and cannot be UNDERSTOOD in the sense of a **psychology of possession** (*Besitzpsychologie*) but only of a **psychology of use** (*Gebrauchspsychologie*) (p. 205).

> INDIVIDUAL PSYCHOLOGY is the **psychology of use** and emphasizes the CREATIVE appropriation and exploitation of all these [hereditary and environmental] influences (p. 205).

> INDIVIDUAL PSYCHOLOGY . . . considers the attitude of an individual to the problems of life in order to UNDERSTAND him, and therefore considers the **use** he makes of his capacities. (p. 205).

> Our objection to the teachings of the hereditarians and every other tendency to overstress the significance of constitutional disposition is that the important thing is not what one is born with, but what **use** one makes of that equipment. We must ask ourselves: "*Who* uses it?" (p. 176).

PSYCHOSIS: "NO!"

The **"No!"** of the **psychotic** expresses his or her departure from the COMMON SENSE of the community into a fantasy world of his or her own CREATION. The **psychotic** operates AS IF to say, "I'll see and do it my way!" He or she does not acknowledge the imperative of communal life (unlike the NEUROTIC, who acknowledges it only to seek excuses from it, and unlike the SOCIOPATH, who acknowledges it only to defy it in a claim of personal SUPERIORITY and exemption). Organic weakness, malfunctioning, or intoxication (where any of these can be identified) appear to facilitate the withdrawal rather than to determine it.

> The patient develops his inner world, which contrasts with reality, in the foundation of a wrong perspective (p. 300).

> **Psychosis** . . . appears to us as the mental suicide of an individual who does not believe himself adequate to the demands of reality and to his own GOALS (p. 323).

THE QUESTION

Adler asked clients a particular question to uncover the purpose of symptoms. Dreikurs emphasized use of this procedure, referring to it as **The Question**. He advocated its use for differential diagnosis (to establish whether or not a symptom pointed to an organic disease process or a functional disturbance). **The Question** is: "How would your life be different if you did not have_____ (the symptom)?" For Dreikurs, if the patient answered that his or her life would be the same, only the symptom would be gone, the answer indicated the likely presence of undiagnosed organic disease. If, however, the client responded that being free of the symptom would mean being able to do something (get a job, get married, move, settle accounts with someone, excel, have a child, etc.), Dreikurs took the answer to mean that the symptom was more likely to represent a functional disorder (Dreikurs, 1973, p. 56). Examples of Adler's use of the technique in treatment follow, below.

> Ask the patient: "What would you do if you were completely well?" Most certainly he will name precisely that demand of society which we would expect him to avoid (p. 332).

> If you want to find out how insomnia fits in with the whole personality, ask the patient: "What would you do if you could sleep?" Then he will tell of what he is afraid (p. 311).

RECOGNITION REFLEX

Dreikurs used the term **recognition reflex** for the sudden smile of **recognition**, laughter, and/or direct gaze meeting the eyes of the counselor when the counselor, testing a hypothesis regarding the purpose of client MOVEMENT, offers an on-target interpretation.

> The **recognition reflex** — an involuntary, spontaneous reaction by the youngster — verifies the accuracy of the counselor's confrontation. . . . The **recognition reflex** appears when the client becomes consciously aware of his/her real intention or GOAL (Grunwald & McAbee, 1998, p. 45).

> I once got a RECOGNITION REFLEX from a client, who laughed when I said, "You're bound and determined to be first, and when you *can't* be first best, you *will* be first worst!" (Robert L. Powers, personal communication, n.d.).

SAFEGUARDING/SAFEGUARDING TENDENCY

Safeguarding refers to the mistaken MOVEMENT of the DISCOURAGED person in thought, FEELING, and action in response to perceived threats to his or her SELF-ESTEEM. **Safeguards** may be expressed in anxiety, panic attacks, or paralysis, more or less severe, and all relative to the individual's degree of DISCOURAGEMENT or diminished sense of SOCIAL FEELING and connectedness. **Safeguarding** may show itself in such forms as a claim to being "above it all," marking time, HESITATION, or retreat, all of which may be understood as similar in function to the defense mechanisms later posited by other psychological systems. In PSYCHOANALYTIC theory the "ego" is protected by certain "mechanisms of defense" from recognizing and having to acknowledge the anti-social instincts of the "id." Adler saw the matter differently: What had to be hidden and unacknowledged were not abhorrent impulses, but the cowardice and retreat of the unprepared person, whose confidence in the face of an imperative task is shaken by thoughts of possible failure. From the subjective sense of the individual, the **safeguard** protects a *pretense* of SUPERIORITY, not guaranteed by COMMON SENSE, in addressing life's ordinary challenges. (Consider Aesop's fable of the fox that, unable to jump high enough to reach a bunch of ripe grapes, walks away dismissing them as sour grapes, so he wouldn't have wanted them anyway.)

Through the **safeguarding tendency** the individual aims at getting rid of the FEELING OF INFERIORITY (pp. 109-110).

I have repeatedly described "**safeguarding tendencies**" as the essential character trait of the NEUROSIS. They are evoked by the oversensitivity of the NEUROTIC and his fear of disparagement and disgrace (p. 109).

Over-valuations of one's own achievements and GOALS serve the same PURPOSE; they are . . . arranged by, and originate in, the exaggerated **safeguarding tendency** against the feeling of being "below" (p. 268).

The SUPERIORITY and **safeguarding** of the patient can be seen from a FICTION which begins with an "if" clause: "If I didn't have . . . (this affliction), I would be the first" (p. 275).

All NEUROTIC symptoms have as their object the task of **safeguarding** the patient's SELF-ESTEEM and thereby also the life-line [LIFESTYLE] (p. 263).

SELF-BOUNDEDNESS (*ICHGEBUNDENHEIT*)

Although it is not part of the Adlerian vocabulary, we include the term here because it is a concept that played an important part in psychoanalytic theory (as well as in the Gestalt therapy movement associated with Fritz Perls, Paul Goodman, and others), and it was singled out by Adler for explicit criticism and rejection. Briefly, **self-boundedness** has been defined as follows:

> Hypothesized lines of demarcation between the ego and 1) the external world (external ego boundary) and 2) the internal world, including the repressed unconscious, the id, and much of the superego (internal ego boundary) (Edgerton and Campbell, 1994, ¶ 1).

In the 1960s **self-boundedness** was expressed in the sentimental individualism of the "Gestalt prayer," ascribed to Perls, beginning, "I do my thing and you do your thing." Perls's associate Paul Goodman also framed his idea of "radical individualism" on the basis of **self-boundedness**, arguing for the free expression of the individual's "needs," postulated as determinants of behavior, including those that give rise to the desire for homosexual contact, which, Goodman maintained, is one of the "human things that we really need" (Goodman, 1969, ¶ 9).

Adler saw such ideas as being organized (more often than not UNCONSCIOUSLY) in ARRANGEMENTS that (in a PRIVATE SENSE) justify MOVEMENT. The implication is disguised, but follows a PRIVATE LOGIC, arguing that my "need" determines the moral obligation of others to meet it. Such arguments facilitate claims to a personal exemption from the universal obligations of mutual respect and support entailed in the SOCIAL EMBEDDEDNESS of human beings. [See EMBEDDEDNESS/SOCIAL EMBEDDEDNESS.]

> Self-boundedness (*Ichgebundenheit*) is the central point of attack of INDIVIDUAL PSYCHOLOGY (p. 112).

> **Self-boundedness** is an artifact thrust upon the child during his EDUCATION and by the present state of our social structure (p. 138).

> The individuality of the child cuts across his physical individuality, it involves a whole CONTEXT of social relations (p.127).

> The style or the pattern of a child's life cannot be understood without reference to the persons who look after him and who make up for his INFERIORITY (p. 127).

> The **self-bound** individual always forgets that his self would be SAFEGUARDED better and automatically the more he prepares himself for the welfare of mankind, and that in this respect no limits are set for him (p. 112).

SELF-ESTEEM/SELF-CONCEPT

Self-esteem is a confidence and satisfaction in oneself, synonymous with self-respect; **self-concept** is the mental image one has of oneself (both, *Merriam Webster's Collegiate Dictionary*, 1993). These terms are related to INFERIORITY FEELING, SUPERIORITY STRIVING, and COMMUNITY FEELING. *Minderwertigkeitsgefühl* is the German word for INFERIORITY FEELING, the feeling of having *diminished worth* or of being of *less value*, a universally experienced sense of limitation and mortality that generally moves people to STRIVE in ways that enhance self and others. This basic awareness of imperfection can also turn people away from COMMON SENSE and CONTRIBUTION, and toward self-aggrandizement, when they are DISCOURAGED, feel disrespected, or sense themselves to be unwelcome in the human community. Adler says, "The sense of worth of the self shall not be allowed to be diminished" (p. 358).

A personal estimate of oneself (**self-concept**) as worthwhile and valuable translates into **self-esteem**. A satisfactory **self-concept** and resulting **self-esteem** derive from **activity** on the USEFUL SIDE of life, that is, in line with COMMUNITY FEELING. (This is not the same as Émile Coué's vacuous, but popular, late 19th and early 20th Century autosuggestion, "Every day in every way, I am getting better and better." The recently flourishing **self-esteem** movement, apparently failing to recognize that a healthy **self-concept** and its consequent **self-esteem** result from enhanced COMMUNITY FEELING and CONTRIBUTION, seemed to promote various types of autosuggestion.) [See LIFE-STYLE.]

> All NEUROTIC symptoms have as their object the task of SAFEGUARDING the patient's **self-esteem** and thereby also the [STYLE OF LIFE] (p. 263).

> The only salvation from the continuously driving INFERIORITY FEELING is the knowledge and the feeling of being valuable which originate from the CONTRIBUTION to the common welfare (p. 155).

> Valuable can mean nothing other than valuable for human society (p. 255).

See Sweeney (1989), pp.47-54.

SELF-IDEAL (*PERSÖNLICHKEITSIDEAL*)

The **self-ideal** (G., *Persönlichkeitsideal*) is an expression of the FICTIONAL GOAL of the personality, which is an image of success, and the organizing principle of the STYLE OF LIVING. Adler introduced the term in *The Neurotic Character* (1912/1928), his first major statement of his system after his separation from the Freudian circle and subsequent to his encounter with Vaihinger's *Philosophy of the 'As If': A System of the Theoretical, Practical, and Religious Fictions of Mankind* (1911/1968). The latter provided him with a schema whereby he could interpret ideas and images of the future as operative in the present field as GUIDELINES and points of orientation, as well as COMPENSATIONS for childhood feelings of weakness and incompleteness. Adler likens the FICTIONAL GOAL of the **self-ideal** to the FICTIONAL meridians and parallels on charts used for orientation. Freud misunderstood and misrepresented Adler's use of **self-ideal**, apparently being unwilling to allow for a dynamic forward movement in psychic life, retaining a backward orientation in his concept of infantile fantasy, and casting "ego ideal" (in contrast to Adler's **self-ideal**) to describe a kind of burden thrust upon a child by parental demands. [See "AS IF" (FICTIONS); FICTIONAL GOAL/GUIDING FICTION/FICTIONAL FINALISM.]

> In every case, the point of the **self-ideal** (*Persönlichkeitsideal*) posited beyond reality remains effective (p. 94).

> The only point we consider fixed is the **personality ideal** (p. 284).

> The fictional, abstract **ideal** is the point of origin for the formation and differentiation of the given psychological resources into preparatory attitudes, readinesses, and character traits. The individual then wears the character traits demanded by his FICTIONAL GOAL, just as the character mask (*persona*) of the ancient actor had to fit the finale of the tragedy (p. 94).

> The GOAL of the mental life of man becomes its governing principle, its *causa finalis* (p. 94).

SEXUALITY

Adler was a member of the famous "Wednesdays," gatherings at Freud's house for discussions of psychology, dominated by assumptions regarding drives, and especially the supremacy of the **sex** drive as posited by Freud. Fourteen years older than Adler, Freud had taken the lead in the new psychology, and was attracting attention for his books on hysteria and DREAMS. Nevertheless, in due course, and especially as they attempted to understand the confluence of the drives in the unity of the personality, Adler and Freud came to radically different conclusions. Adler proposed the AGGRESSION DRIVE as giving direction to the other drives, and so saw **sexual** desire as included in the active (aggressive) forward MOVEMENT of the individual. Freud remained convinced of the superordinate role of the **sex** drive, which he saw as pressing all the other drives into the service of its satisfaction. Adler came to repudiate the idea of biological drives altogether, as well as the primacy of **sex** in the psyche. Considering the **sexual** function in the service of EVOLUTION and the survival of the species, Adler located the conjunctive **sexual** FEELING and behavior
in the realm of LOVE and intimacy (and their problems). As such it is one of the TASKS OF LIFE assigned to each individual by the logic of social living. We are born into one of the two **sexes** (or one of the so-called inter-sexual anomalies [see Fausto-Sterling, 1993]) and not the other (or any one of the others); therefore, each person, in his or her own CREATIVE way, must decide how to make use of **sexuality**, either in COOPERATIVE intimacy on the USEFUL SIDE OF LIFE, or on the socially USELESS
SIDE in exploitive ARRANGEMENTS.

Adler was a FEMINIST, uncompromising concerning the necessity for EQUALITY between the **sexes**, especially in the sphere of LOVE and intimacy. In a period when homosexual love and other adaptations outside the heterosexual norm were punishable crimes, he instead considered these to be (using the scientific language of that age) *perversions*, or "wrong turns," and therefore in need of correction. (However, Adler is said to have had a colleague present the case of a patient who had revealed in the course of treatment that he was homosexual, asking what Adler thought he should do with him. "Is he happy?" Adler asked. Upon receiving an affirmative reply, he continued "Well then, why don't we leave him alone?"). [See LOVE AND MARRIAGE; EQUALITY; FEMINISM.]

> **Sexuality** is a 'twosomeness' [G., *Zweisamkeit*], the achievement of two equal partners (Adler, 1978, p. 322).

> Human **sex** is not merely a biological urge, but a function which can be used according to the individual's intentions (Dreikurs, 1973, p. 246).

> We do not know what development **sexuality** would take if we would not, and would not have to, set up barriers against it (Adler, 1978, p. 365).

> [As concerns disturbances], most frequently we find within the **sexual** relationship the erroneous assumption that LOVE is an obligation for the other party (Adler, 1978, p. 110).

> The dialect of the **sexual** organs is especially expressive. . . . [In practically every case] the patient is expressing, by the disorder of his [or her] **sexual** functioning, a stoppage, hesitation, or escape (p. 312).

> [Persons who] deviate from the general expectation are mostly persons who face the LOVE problem with extreme hesitation and prejudices, are afraid of their **sexual** partner and, therefore, are looking for a partner in whom they suspect less POWER and strength (Adler, 1978, p. 111-112).

> In a normal STYLE OF LIFE, **sex** will find its proper expression (Adler, 1978, p. 82).

93

SIBLING RIVALRY (COMPETITION)

In a section titled "Stay out of Fights!" in his popular book on PARENTING, *Children: The Challenge* (1964), Dreikurs recounts the story of a put-upon first-born son whose younger brother and baby sister constantly got him into trouble through their provocations and his retaliatory responses to them. The brother had taken the position of "the good one," while the youngest, allied with the second-born, played "baby girl" (complete with displays of WATER POWER). The parents were, of course, blind to the children's maneuvers. They knew only that their first-born was a "bad boy," in need of constant rebukes for abusing his siblings, until Dreikurs revealed what was really going on. This case of **sibling rivalry** uncovers the role of PARENTS who may naively add to the trouble they complain of having with the children. There is, of course, **rivalry** among children under different circumstances, especially between the first two children, and more especially in families in which the PARENTS are jockeying for position or openly vying to see who will rule. Later-born children may also feel challenged by their siblings: There is no position without its advantages and its disadvantages [see PSYCHOLOGICAL BIRTH-ORDER POSITION/BIRTH-ORDER VANTAGE]. Each child enters a world that is already inhabited, and each must fit in and stand out by MAKING A PLACE for him- or herself among the others. Sometimes this eventuates in **rivalry,** sometimes in **competition**.

According to Powers (one of the present authors), a student and later colleague in Dreikurs's practice, Dreikurs differentiated between direct and indirect **competition** by observing that direct **competition** is seen when siblings struggle to outdo each other in the *same* arena, while indirect **competition** operates when siblings try to distinguish themselves in *separate* arenas. For example, a younger sibling who enjoys and is friends with a senior sibling, and does not want to challenge him or her directly, may turn his attention to another domain of activity. If the elder is an athlete, the younger may become an academic. It is generally helpful to remember that children are not likely to compete for the position of second-best in any arena. [See MAKING/TAKING/FINDING A PLACE FOR ONESELF; MISTAKEN GOALS OF THE DISCOURAGED CHILD; PARENTING.]

See PARENTING for suggested texts in child guidance.

SOCIAL ADAPTATION/SOCIAL ADJUSTMENT

Adler made extensive use of the idea of EVOLUTION, incorporating its implications in his UNDERSTANDING of human being. This is exemplified in his concept of SUPERIORITY STRIVING and in his theories concerning EQUALITY and SOCIAL INTEREST. (See MENTAL ILLNESS: ADLER'S UNITARY (UNIFIED) THEORY.) **Adaptation** and **adjustment** are therefore (in his vocabulary) to be UNDERSTOOD as pointed to the continuing development and furtherance of the entire human community in its continuing EVOLUTION, *sub specie aeternitatis*.

> The views of INDIVIDUAL PSYCHOLOGY demand the unconditional reduction of STRIVING for power and the development of SOCIAL INTEREST. The watchword of INDIVIDUAL PSYCHOLOGY is the fellow man and the fellowman attitude to the immanent demands of human society (p. 114).

> All social movements . . . should be judged only in accordance with their ability to further interest in our fellow men (p. 449).

> We must connect our thought with a continuous active **adaptation** to the demands of the outer world. . . . This coercion to carry out a better **adaptation** can never end. . . . I am referring to **adaptation** *sub specie aeternitatis* [under the aspect of eternity — Spinoza], for only that bodily and psychological development is "right" which can be deemed right for the future (p. 106).

> We are approaching a time where everyone will take his place as an EQUAL, self-reliantly and freely, no longer in the service of a person, but in the service of a common idea, the idea of physical and mental progress (p. 55).

> The goal of INDIVIDUAL PSYCHOLOGY is *social* **adjustment**

> [Maladjustment arises in cases of] increased INFERIORITY FEELINGS within the first five years of childhood and . . . a lack of SOCIAL INTEREST and COURAGE, the quest for strongest proof of SUPERIORITY, a new problem which is frightening [the EXOGENOUS FACTOR], the patient's DISTANCE from the problem, the exclusion tendency of the patient [narrowing one's sphere of activity, p. 277], [and] his quest for specious relief on the USELESS SIDE, that is, for the *semblance* of SUPERIORITY and not for overcoming difficulties [italics added] (p. 157).

SOCIOPATHY: "NOT ME!"

"Not me!" is Adlerian shorthand for the attitude of the **sociopathic** or fundamentally exploitive, character-disordered individual who engages in "intentional injury of others for [his or her] own advantage" (p. 411). The criminal sees what life requires by way of COOPERATION, but acts as if the requirements are for others (whom the criminal disparages as "suckers") and not for him- or herself. Such a person rationalizes an exemption from the COMMON SENSE by thinking (for example), "I am too smart," or "I am special." The **sociopath** acts AS IF to say, "Yes, *you* should do the right thing," but **"Not me!"** in response to the universal obligations of social living.

> The criminal differs from other failures in one point: he retains a certain amount of activity, which he throws on the USELESS SIDE OF LIFE. . . . Lack of SOCIAL INTEREST, already in the child, will assume a variety of colors depending on whether he takes an active or passive attitude toward life. Even in a passive way, he can expect everything from others; but if he shows more activity he will take from others for himself whatever he wants (p. 413).

> Crime is a coward's imitation of heroism. . . . All criminals are actually cowards. They are evading problems they do not feel strong enough to solve. . . . They like to believe that they are heroes; but this is their mistaken SCHEMA OF APPERCEPTION, a failure of COMMON SENSE (p. 414).

> Criminals have a form of logic which does not take into consideration the rights of the community. From this point of view it is quite all right simply to take something if they just want it, regardless of all the hardship and sorrow that they may inflict upon others. History gives many examples of such criminals who have been leaders of nations (Adler, Alexandra, 1973, p. 46).

SOFT DETERMINISM/SELF-DETERMINISM

Soft determinism expresses the view that individuals are neither produced by HEREDITY nor shaped by ENVIRONMENTAL PRESS. Rather, "genetic possibility and environmental opportunity" (Powers and Griffith, 1987, p. 164) are understood as elements of the situation in which the individual CREATES his or her own unique STYLE OF LIVING. For Adler, the important question was, "What meaning does the individual give to the particularities of his or her situation?" Therefore, **soft determinism** can be thought of as **self-determinism**. [See CREATIVE POWER.]

> It is neither HEREDITY nor ENVIRONMENT which determines [the individual's] relationship to the outside. HEREDITY only endows him with certain abilities. ENVIRONMENT only gives him certain impressions. These abilities and impressions . . . [and] the interpretations he makes of [his] experiences are the bricks which he uses in his own "CREATIVE" way in building up his attitude toward life (p. 206).

> What matters ultimately is what the child, the individual, does with the equipment he inherits (p. 206).

> There are no reasons for the development of character; rather, a child can make use of experiences for his GOAL and turn them into reasons (p. 209).

> It is not the child's experiences which dictate his actions; it is the conclusions he draws from his experiences (p. 209).

> HEREDITY and ENVIRONMENTAL factors play a part only in the sense of providing a certain probability (p. 164).

> Meanings are not determined by situations, but we **determine ourselves** by the meanings we give to situations (Adler, 1980, p. 14).

> We are *self-determined* by the meaning we give to our experiences (Adler, 1980, p. 14).

SPITTING IN THE SOUP/BESMIRCH A CLEAN CONSCIENCE

According to Dreikurs, Adler used these homely metaphors to characterize the process of exposing to clients what they are actually *doing*, in order to make these actions distasteful to them. It is a way to spoil the **clean conscience** of the client, who may, of course, choose to continue in the mistaken MOVEMENT, but who can no longer do so innocently. [See PARADOX/ANTI-SUGGESTION.]

> To motivate reorientation, I employ a mirror technique, confronting the patient with his GOALS and intentions. . . . When the patient begins to recognize his GOALS, his own conscience becomes a motivating factor. Adler called this process **"spitting in the patient's soup"** (Dreikurs, 1973, p. 12).

> This is a vivid phrase for describing what happens when we expose the hidden agenda or GOAL for [the client's] self-defeating behavior. When the counselor is accurate with his/her observation . . . and can illustrate this clearly . . . [the client] may continue with this behavior but "it won't taste so sweet" (Sweeney, 1989, p. 262).

> [To "**smirch a clean conscience**"] I might say, "Write in capital letters over your bed: 'Every morning I must torment my family as much as possible.' Thus in future you have to do CONSCIOUSLY, and with a bad **conscience**, what you formerly did unaware but with a **clean conscience**." None of my patients has ever followed advice such as this (p. 398).

SUPERIORITY STRIVING/GOAL STRIVING/SUPERIORITY COMPLEX

An appreciation for the evolutionary struggle of all living things to adapt successfully inspired Adler to apply the concept of **superiority striving** to the UNDERSTANDING of human being. He saw the GOAL of success as drawing the individual forward toward mastery and the OVERCOMING of obstacles. He observed that, for socially-interested individuals, the GOAL of **superiority** is on the USEFUL SIDE OF LIFE and contributes to the developing human community. By contrast, the DISCOURAGED person, operating on the USELESS SIDE OF LIFE under the burden of increased FEELINGS OF INFERIORITY, makes the ERROR of supposing that his or her task is to attain a position of **superiority** *over others*. This MOVEMENT invites the antagonism of others, creates a disturbance in the life of the community, and contributes to his or her further defeat. The DISCOURAGED person may express the **superiority striving** in postures of self-elevation, DEPRECIATION of others, and self-aggrandizement, countering the immense FEELINGS OF INFERIORITY with a pattern of COMPENSATORY pretenses to **superiority** which may be termed a **superiority complex**. [Adler, a witty aphorist, conveyed some of his ideas in humorous metaphors. One of his biographers, Phyllis Bottome (1939) reports this anecdote: "What is man," he once said to a friend of his, "but a drop of water. A conceited drop," he added after a slight pause (p. 119).]

> The whole of human life proceeds along this great line of action — from below to above, from minus to plus, from defeat to victory (p. 255).

> It is the **striving for superiority** which is behind every human CREATION and it is the source for all CONTRIBUTIONS which are made to our culture (p. 255).

> [**Superiority striving**] can take place in a satisfactory way and can lead to a proper feeling of worth only on the USEFUL SIDE, in the developed SOCIAL INTEREST, where the individual senses himself as valuable. Valuable can mean nothing other than valuable for human society (pp. 254-255).

> When individuals — both children and adults — feel weak, they cease to be interested socially, but **strive** for [personal] **superiority** (p. 260).

> [The **superiority complex**] is a COMPENSATION for the INFERIORITY COMPLEX (p. 260).

> We must bear in mind, of course, that the word **complex** as attached to INFERIORITY and **superiority** merely represents an exaggerated condition of the SENSE OF INFERIORITY and the **striving for superiority** (p. 259).

> The origin of humanity and the ever-repeated beginning of infant life impresses with every psychological act: Achieve! Arise! Conquer (p. 103).

TELEOLOGY/PURPOSE

The terms **teleology, purpose**, FINALISM are used by those who study behavior as moving toward ends or GOALS. The word **teleology** derives from the Greek *telos*, meaning "end." INDIVIDUAL PSYCHOLOGY considers all behavior (thought, FEELING, and action) as **purposive**, that is, as MOVEMENT in line with the individual's LIFE-STYLE GOALS (whether or not the **purpose** of the MOVEMENT is CONSCIOUSLY UNDERSTOOD by the individual). [See GUIDING FICTION/FICTIONAL GOAL/FICTIONAL FINALISM.]

INDIVIDUAL PSYCHOLOGY insists absolutely on the indispensability of FINALISM for the understanding of all psychological phenomena. Causes, powers, instincts, impulses, and the like cannot serve as explanatory principles. The final GOAL alone can (p. 92).

The science of INDIVIDUAL PSYCHOLOGY developed out of the effort to UNDERSTAND that mysterious CREATIVE POWER of life which expresses itself in the desire to develop, to STRIVE, to achieve, and even to COMPENSATE for defeats in one direction by STRIVING for success in another. This power is *teleological,* it expresses itself in the STRIVING after a GOAL, and, in this STRIVING, every bodily and psychological MOVEMENT is made to COOPERATE (p. 92).

Every individual acts and suffers in accordance with his peculiar **teleology**, which has all the inevitability of fate, so long as he does not UNDERSTAND it (p. 93).

The fictional GOAL is blurred and pliable; it cannot be measured; it has been constructed with inadequate and definitely ungifted powers. It has no real existence and therefore cannot be completely comprehended causally. But it can well be understood as a **teleological** device of the soul which seeks orientation. This **teleology** is self-imposed. It arises in the psychological organ and must be understood as a device and as the individual's own construction (p. 93).

100

TRAINING, SELF-TRAINING, AND THE REHEARSAL OF CHARACTER

INDIVIDUAL PSYCHOLOGY understands the development of the STYLE OF LIVING as arising in the CONTEXT of (a) childhood **training** by those in the family of origin (parents, siblings, and others in the household); (b) the **self-training** of the child who tests his or her sense of how to MAKE A PLACE in the family on the basis of his or her developing opinions; and (c) the child's **rehearsal** of those convictions and operations which the child experiences as effective, whether on the USEFUL or USELESS SIDE OF LIFE.

> Wherever we find an ability it is the result of an interest in which the child has **trained** himself, stimulated by the totality of his circumstances (p. 430).

> [The child] strives within the incalculable realm of his possibilities. From trial and error a **training** results for the child and a general way [of moving] towards a GOAL of perfection which appears to offer him fulfillment (p. 187).

> From the beginning of a child's life a **training** comes about, as a result of which the child permits the growth of a role within himself of which he may be CONSCIOUS or UNCONSCIOUS (p. 367).

> I am convinced of the free CREATIVE POWER of the individual in his earliest childhood and of his restricted power in later life, once the child has given himself a fixed LAW OF MOVEMENT for his life (p. 186).

> [The child] arrives at his LAW OF MOVEMENT which aids him after a certain amount of **training** to obtain a STYLE OF LIFE, in accordance with which we see the individual thinking, FEELING, and acting throughout his whole life (p. 188).

> You cannot **train** or condition a living being for defeat (p. 167).

TWO POINTS ON A LINE

Dinkmeyer, Dinkmeyer, and Sperry (1987) define **two points on a line** as finding "an imaginary line that connects someone's two apparently contradictory . . . [behaviors]. This makes it possible to locate innumerable other characteristics along the same line." They provide the example of a woman who, on the one hand, was good as gold and who, on the other, threw tantrums. The therapist hypothesized that "she wanted to be the best and if she couldn't be the best at being good, she would try to be the best at being bad." The woman felt immediately understood, and remembered that in childhood her father had told her that when she was good, she was very, very good and when she was bad she was horrid (p. 268).

> We have made the important contention that the UNDERSTANDING of human nature can never be learned by the examination of isolated phenomena which have been withdrawn from their entire psychic CONTEXT and relationships. It is essential for this UNDERSTANDING that we compare at least **two phenomena** which are separated by as great a time as possible and connect them within a unified pattern" (Adler, 1957, p.152).

> Dreikurs used an analogy from geometry applied to the LIFESTYLE concept. "One needs **two points** to draw a line, and once a line is drawn, one knows an infinite number of points." If a client reveals two apparently independent and contrary facts, a line of logic can be drawn to delineate a picture of a unified, self-consistent LIFE STYLE. The counselor attempts to find the line of logic through intelligent GUESSING, and if correct, the answer will resolve the puzzle and indicate the basic LIFE STYLE (Terner & Pew, 1978, p. 247).

TYPES/TENDENCIES/THEMES/PRIORITIES

Considering each individual as a UNIQUE VARIANT of human possibility, Adler was reluctant to speak of **types.** Even so, he once did say, "for teaching purposes only, to illuminate the broad field . . . we shall designate here four different **types** in order temporarily to classify the attitude and behavior of individuals toward outside problems" (p. 167). He identified (a) the dominant or ruling **type,** (b) the avoiding **type,** (c) the getting or dependent **type,** and (d) the socially USEFUL **type.** The first three describe those not properly or adequately prepared to meet life's requirements. In varying degrees they resist having to COOPERATE, are reluctant to CONTRIBUTE in equitable give and take, and suffer the feeling of being misfitted. The socially USEFUL **type** is characterized by a willingness to COOPERATE, to CONTRIBUTE, and to be active for him- or herself in ways that are to some extent of benefit to others. [For a critique of **typologies,** see Powers and Griffith, 1996.]

Kefir and Corsini (1974) report on eight different **typologies** before distilling from these their **typology** of four features, stating, "As psychotherapists we are most concerned with the person's general disposition, that is to say his central **tendency,**" which they arrive at by means of a triangular chart. The center represents a neutral zone, while the points represent accord, conflict, and evasion. The therapist or the client places indicators on the triangle to show the client's present social interactions, and other indicators to show where the client would like to be, so that a graphic display of the client's "central **tendencies**" and GOALS emerge for further work.

Mosak (1977), referring to Adler's ability to capture major **themes** in patients' LIFESTYLES, studied the interrelatedness of the LIFESTYLES of clients whose "LIFESTYLE convictions, at certain points, hamper the individual in coping with the LIFE TASKS." He searched for "common elements," using observation and analysis of client movement, psychological testing, and EARLY RECOLLECTIONS, on the basis of which he proposed a classification of eight representative "central **themes**" (pp. 138, 141).

Manaster and Corsini (1982) report on the four "personality **priorities**" (controller, avoider, being superior or judging others, and pleaser) proposed by Nira Kefir in 1972, arguing that these are not personality GOALS, but attitudes and behaviors created and practiced as SAFEGUARDS of the self-esteem that arise as protection against the repetition of an earlier "traumatic event" (an "impasse" or threatening situation), whose recurrence is warded off by means of the **priority** (p. 141).

> The principles which guide us when grouping individuals into these four **types** [dominant, avoiding, getting, and socially USEFUL] are the degree of their approach to social integration and the form of MOVEMENT which they develop . . . to achieve success (in their own interpretation) (p. 168).

> INDIVIDUAL PSYCHOLOGY recognizes . . . that each individual must be studied in the light of his own peculiar development. To present the individual UNDERSTANDABLY, in words, requires an extensive reviewing of all his facets. Yet too often psychologists are tempted away from this recognition to take the easier but unfruitful roads of classification (p. 167).

> We do not consider human beings as **types,** because every person has an individual STYLE OF LIFE. If we speak of **types,** therefore, it is only as a conceptual device to make more understandable the similarities of individuals (p. 166).

> The classification of **types** can thus be . . . a source of confusion if we do not realize that **types** are merely convenient abstractions. A human being cannot be **typed** or classified (p. 167).

> Paltry **typologies** tell us nothing about the individual mistake (p. 196).

USEFUL vs. USELESS SIDE OF LIFE

Individuals who operate on the **useful side of life** COOPERATE with the community, at once advancing themselves and the community toward improved ADAPTATION. Those on the **useless side of life** operate in ways that are obstructive of or antithetical to the interests and well-being of the developing human community for the sake of what they mistakenly believe to be personal advantage.

> The really important differences of conduct are . . . those of . . . **useful** and **useless**. By **useful** I mean in the interests of mankind generally. The most sensible estimate of the value of any activity is its helpfulness to all mankind, present and future, a criterion that applies not only to that which subserves the immediate preservation of life, but also the higher activities such as religion, science, and art. It is true that we cannot always decide what is strictly worthwhile from this point of view. But [the more] . . . we are guided by the impulse to act **usefully** . . . the nearer we approach to true perception (Adler, 1964b, p. 78).

> There is only one reason for an individual to side-step to the **useless side**: the fear of a defeat on the **useful side** (p. 157).

> Only those are able to muster the COURAGE to advance on the **useful side** who consider themselves a part of the whole, who are at home on this earth and in this mankind (p. 159).

> They [the NEUROTIC and criminal] have lost COURAGE . . . to proceed on the **useful side of life**. . . . They have turned away from the real problems of life (p. 255).

> [STRIVING] can take place in a satisfactory way and can lead to a proper feeling of worth only on the **useful side**, in the developed SOCIAL INTEREST where the individual senses himself as valuable. Valuable can mean nothing other than valuable for human society (pp. 254-255).

WATER POWER

Water power describes the use of tears to prevail against opposition, a tactic employed by those who believe themselves (and who are believed to be) weak, in their conflicts with those who are presumed to be strong.

> When the pampered individual has tried out a certain method and found it successful, he will use it again and again. If a certain symptom is selected in childhood and found workable, the NEUROTIC adult will often employ it in his later life as a means of furthering his asocial ends (p. 288).

> Whether the NEUROTIC dominates by bullying or by whining will depend on his TRAINING: he will choose the device which he has tested best and found most effective for his purposes (p. 288).

> The DISCOURAGED child who finds that he can tyrannize best by tears will be a cry-baby; and a direct line of development leads from the cry-baby to the adult depressed patient. Tears and complaints — the means which I have called **"water power"** — can be an extremely useful weapon for disturbing COOPERATION and reducing others to a condition of slavery (p. 288).

WILL TO POWER

The idea of a **will to power**, attributed (mistakenly) to Friedrich Nietzsche (1844-1900), was widely influential in Adler's time, but more as a phrase than a clearly defined concept with an agreed-upon meaning. Briefly, it appealed to those working to understand the general processes of nature in the light of the implications of EVOLUTION and the emergence of living things, without appealing to divine agency and intention. Thus, the conservative claim, previously put forward as unarguable, that "self-preservation is the first law of life," was challenged by progressive images of the "life force" as aggressively dynamic and expansive, AS IF pressing toward a better and stronger ADAPTATION. [See HISTORICAL CONTEXT: ADLER IN HIS TIME.] By 1908, early in his effort to amend drive (G., *Trieb*) (or instinct) theory, before his ultimate departure from it, Adler posited "AGGRESSION" as the central organizing principle in the "confluence of drives," a dramatic first step away from dualism toward HOLISM. The next step in this course of change, postulating the MASCULINE PROTEST as a STRIVING toward SELF-ESTEEM, and a SAFEGUARD against humiliation and defeat, was decisive. It marked Adler's abandonment of efforts to use the language of drives. (His break with Freud was the unavoidable consequence.) [See H. L. and R. R. Ansbacher (1964a, pp. 34ff.) for a detailed review of this history.]

In his first major text, *The Neurotic Character,* published in 1912, Adler continued to use the language of AGGRESSION, and to associate his UNDERSTANDING of human STRIVING with Nietzsche's **"will to power"** and "will to seem," *especially* in describing exaggerated forms of NEUROTIC STRIVING. [See the first quotation, below.] He came to regret this, and later claimed that he meant the comparison to apply *only* in this area and not in the generally more useful forms of the universal SUPERIORITY STRIVING toward completeness or perfection. But the harm was done: The association of Adler to Nietzsche and notions of power continues to impair an understanding of Adler's development, and impedes a wider and more serious consideration of his work.

In fairness to Nietzsche, it must be said that he had an unrealized ambition to develop the implications of the term **"will to power,"** which, after his death was claimed as a project by his anti-Semitic sister. By the 1930s, connected to assumptions foreign to Nietzsche's thinking, the term was distorted in arguments to support Nazi pseudo-philosophy. [See AGGRESSION DRIVE]

> Much of our view of the enhancement of the SELF-ESTEEM as the GUIDING FICTION is included in Nietzsche's **"will to power"** and "will to seem". . . . We wish to point out the absolute primacy of the **will to power**, a GUIDING FICTION which asserts itself the more forcibly and is developed the earlier, often precipitously, the stronger the INFERIORITY FEELING of the ORGANICALLY INFERIOR child comes to the foreground (p. 111).

> Regarding the STRIVING for **power**, we find the misunderstanding that INDIVIDUAL PSYCHOLOGY not only regards psychological life as the STRIVING for **power**, but propagates this idea. This STRIVING for **power** is not our madness, it is what we find in others (p. 113).

> The STRIVING of each actively moving individual is toward OVERCOMING, not towards **power**. . . . STRIVING for **power** — better, for personal **power** — represents only one of a thousand TYPES, all of which seek perfection, a security-giving PLUS situation (Adler, 1979, p. 275).

Footnotes

[1]Bruner, Jerome S. (1951). Personality dynamics and the process of perceiving. In R. R. Blake & G.V. Ramsey (Eds.), *Perception: An approach to personality* (pp. 121-147), New York: Ronald Press. "I find it hard to decide whether I have been discussing the role of personality factors in the process of perceiving or the role of perceptual factors in personality functioning" (p. 145).

[2]We are grateful to Atul Gawande, M. D., and his research assistant, Katy Thompson, at the Harvard School of Public Health, for forwarding to us their email from Kaare Christensen of Southern Denmark University reporting the following: "The exact number for the mean difference in lifespan for monozygotic twins born in Denmark in 1870-1900 and surviving to at least age 6 is 15.2 years (compared to 18.2 for dizygotic twins)." [KChristensen@health.sdu.dk].

[3]Research conducted by Avshalom Caspi, M. D., of the Institute of Psychiatry in London, reporting in *The Week* magazine (September 19, 2003, p. 20), suggests that one's basic personality is fixed by age three. Caspi and others interviewed 1,000 children at age three, grouping them into five categories (confident, well-adjusted, reserved, inhibited, and restless), and found in a reassessment 23 years later that the now-adult subjects could be similarly characterized. Dr. Caspi states, "The message is that parents and teachers should not ignore what they see in a 3-year-old as a passing phase."

[4]In two loosely written sketches, apparently meant to be taken as preliminary, H. H. Mosak with R. Dreikurs (1973) proposed two further LIFE TASKS, namely: a fourth, "to get along with oneself" or "coping with oneself"; and a fifth, alluded to as a task that "may go under several names – the spiritual, the EXISTENTIAL, the search for meaning, the metaphysical, the metapsychological, and the ontological." These proposals appear to rest on grave misunderstandings of Adler's INDIVIDUAL PSYCHOLOGY. A self "getting along with" or "coping with" another self predicates a dualism and intrapsychic conflict that is incongruent with the UNITY and indivisibility of Adler's construct of the unique STYLE OF LIVING. As for claiming to identify a TASK that "may go under several names," none of which is defined, and each of which may carry implications foreign to any or all of the others, we can only observe that the incoherence of such a statement rules out any serious discussion of it. Finally, Adler's image of the three LIFE TASKS, and its analogy to life as a schoolteacher handing out assignments, includes his idea that each of the three problems confronting every human being is dependent upon COOPERATION for its solution. Neither of the TASKS proposed by Mosak with Dreikurs can be seen in this way; instead, each is a private, internal matter, and therefore either may serve as a personal preoccupation and exemption from correction by the COMMON SENSE. [See Powers & Griffith, 1996.]

[5]In a personal letter to Robert L. Powers of July 3, 1986, Heinz L. Ansbacher wrote, "I also find your neologism of [the] PSYCHO-CLARITY process quite acceptable. Your approach is far more Adlerian than that of many 'Adlerians' who are actually reifiers and whose thinking is in fact quite elementaristic."

[6]Tim Flannery, in a review of *The tree: A natural history of what trees are, how they live, and why they matter* by Colin Tudge (New York: Crown, 2006), writes, "Living tissue, [Tudge] says, 'is constantly replacing itself, even when it seems to stay the same. It is not a thing but a performance.'" (*The New York Review of Books,* February 15, 2007, p. 35).

Selected Resources in Adlerian Psychology

General texts

Adler, A. (1964). *The Individual Psychology of Alfred Adler: A systematic presentation in selections from his writings.* (H. L. Ansbacher & R. R. Ansbacher, Eds.). New York: Harper Torchbooks.

Adler, A. (1979). *Superiority and social interest; A collection of later writings* (2nd Rev. ed.). (H. L. Ansbacher & R. R. Ansbacher, Eds.). New York: Viking/Compass. (Original work published 1964)

Adler, A. (1982). *Cooperation between the sexes: Writings on women and men, love and marriage, and sexuality.* (H. L. Ansbacher & R. R. Ansbacher, Eds.). New York: Norton. (Original work published 1978)

Carlson, J., Watts, R. E., & Maniacci, M. P. (2006). *Adlerian therapy: Theory and practice.* Washington, DC: American Psychological Association.

Dinkmeyer, D., Jr., & Sperry, L. (2000). *Counseling and psychotherapy: An integrated Individual Psychology approach* (3rd ed.). Upper Saddle River, NJ: Prentice-Hall.

Dreikurs, R. (1949). *Fundamentals of Adlerian Psychology* (Rev. ed.). Chicago: Alfred Adler Institute. (Original work published 1933)

Manaster, G. J., & Corsini, R. J. (1982). *Individual Psychology: Theory and practice.* Itasca, IL: F. E. Peacock.

Oberst, U. E., & Stewart, A. E. (2003). *Adlerian psychotherapy: An advanced approach to Individual Psychology.* New York: Brunner-Routledge.

Sweeney, T. J. (1989). *Adlerian counseling: A practical approach for a new decade* (3rd ed.). Muncie, IN: Accelerated Development.

Specialized Texts

Clark, A. J. (2002). *Early recollections: Theory and practice in counseling and psychotherapy.* New York: Brunner-Routledge.

Dreikurs, R. (with Soltz, V.). (1964). *Children: The challenge.* New York: Hawthorn/Dutton.

Dreikurs, R., Grunwald, B. B., & Pepper, F. C. (1971). *Maintaining sanity in the classroom: Illustrated teaching techniques.* New York: Harper & Row.

Dreikurs, S. E. (1986) Cows can be purple. (N. Catlin & J. W. Croake, Eds.). Chicago: Alfred Adler Institute.

Grunwald, B. B., & McAbee, H. V. (1999). *Guiding the family* (2nd ed.). Philadelphia: Accelerated Development.

Kopp, R. R. (1995). *Metaphor therapy: Using client-generated metaphors in psychotherapy.* New York: Brunner/Mazel.

Kottman, T. (2001). *Play therapy: Basics and beyond.* Alexandria, VA: American Counseling Association.

McKay, G. D, & Maybell, S. A. (2004). *Calming the family storm: Anger management for moms, dads, and all the kids.* Atascadero, CA: Impact.

Selected Resources in Adlerian Psychology (cont'd)

Mosak, H. H., & Maniacci, M. P. (1998). *Tactics in counseling and psychotherapy.* Itasca, IL: F. E. Peacock.

Nelsen, J. (1996). *Positive discipline.* New York: Ballantine.

Powers, R. L., & Griffith, J. (1987). *Understanding life-style: The psycho-clarity process.* Port Townsend, WA: Adlerian Psychology Associates.

Sonstegard, M. A., & Bitter, J. R. (with Pelonis, P.). (2004). *Adlerian group counseling and therapy: Step-by-step.* New York: Brunner-Routledge.

Sperry, L., & Carlson, J. (1993). *Psychopathology and psychotherapy from diagnosis to treatment.* Muncie, IN: Accelerated Development.

Starr, A. (1977). *Psychodrama: Rehearsal for living.* Chicago: Nelson-Hall.

Collections

Carlson, J., & Slavik, S. (Eds.). (1997). *Techniques in Adlerian Psychology.* Washington, DC: Accelerated Development.

Christensen, O. C. (Ed.). (2004). *Adlerian family counseling: A manual for counselor, educator, and psychotherapist* (3rd ed.). Minneapolis, MN: Educational Media.

Dreikurs, R. (1973). *Psychodynamics, psychotherapy and counseling: Collected papers* (Rev. ed.). Chicago: Alfred Adler Institute.

Kern, R. M., Hawes, E. C., & Christensen, O. C. (Eds.). (1989). *Couples therapy: An Adlerian perspective.* Minneapolis, MN: Educational Media.

Mosak, H. H. (1977). *On purpose: Collected papers.* Chicago: Adler School of Professional Psychology.

Shulman, B. H. (1973). *Contributions to Individual Psychology: Selected papers.* Chicago: Alfred Adler Institute.

Stein, H. (2002). (Series Ed.). *The collected clinical works of Alfred Adler, Vols. 1-10.* (C. Koen, Trans.). San Francisco: Alfred Adler Institute of San Francisco.

Watts, R. E., & Carlson, J. (Eds.). (1999). *Interventions and strategies in counseling and psychotherapy.* Philadelphia: Accelerated Development.

Biographies

Hoffman, E. (1994). *The drive for self: Alfred Adler and the founding of Individual Psychology.* Reading, MA: Addison-Wesley.

Terner, J., & Pew, W. L. (1978). *The courage to be imperfect: The life and work of Rudolf Dreikurs.* New York: Hawthorn.

References

Ellenberger, H. F. (1970). *The discovery of the unconscious: The history and evolution of dynamic psychiatry* (pp. 571-656). New York: Harper Colophon.

Mosak, H. H., & Mosak, B. (1975). *A bibliography for Adlerian Psychology*, Vol. 1; Mosak, B. & Mosak, H. H. (1985), Vol. 2. Washington, DC: Hemisphere.

REFERENCES

Aanstoos, C., Serlin, I., & Greening, T. (2000). History of Division 32, Humanistic Psychology, of the American Psychological Association. In D. Dewsbury (Ed.), *Unification through division: Histories of the divisions of the American Psychological Association*, Vol. V. Retrieved April 9, 2007, from http://en.wikipedia.org/wiki/Humanistic Psychology

Adler, Alexandra. (1973). *Guiding human misfits: A practical application of Adlerian Psychology*. Millwood, NY: Kraus Reprints. (Original work published 1939)

Adler, A. (1917). *Study of organ inferiority and its psychical compensation*. New York: Nervous & Mental Diseases. (Original work published 1907)

Adler, A. (1930). *The education of children*. (E. Jensen & F. Jensen, Trans.). New York: Greenberg.

Adler, A. (1935). Introduction: The fundamental views of Individual Psychology. *International Journal of Individual Psychology, 1*(1), 3-8.

Adler, A. (1957). *Understanding human nature*. (W. B. Wolfe, Trans.). New York: Fawcett. (Original work published 1927)

Adler, A. (1959). *The practice and theory of Individual Psychology*. (P. Radin, Trans.). Paterson, NJ: Littlefield, Adams.

Adler, A. (1963). *The problem child: The life style of the difficult child as analyzed in specific cases*. (G. Daniels, Trans.). New York: Capricorn. (Original work published 1930)

Adler, A. (1964a). *The Individual Psychology of Alfred Adler: A systematic presentation in selections from his writing*. (H. L. Ansbacher & R. R. Ansbacher, Eds.). New York: Harper Torchbooks. (Original work published 1956)

Adler, A. (1964b). *Problems of neurosis*. (P. Mairet, Ed.). New York: Harper & Row. (Original work published 1929)

Adler, A. (1969). *The science of living*. (H. L. Ansbacher, Ed.). New York: Doubleday. (Original work published 1929)

Adler, A. (1978). *Cooperation between the sexes: Writings on women, love and marriage, sexuality and its disorders* (468 pp.). (H. L. Ansbacher & R. R. Ansbacher, Eds. and Trans.). New York: Doubleday. [Also see Adler, A. (1982). *Cooperation between the sexes: Writings on women and men, love and marriage, and sexuality* (184 pp.). (H. L. Ansbacher and R. R. Ansbacher, Eds. and Trans.). New York: Norton.]

Adler, A. (1979). *Superiority and social interest: A collection of later writings* (3rd Rev. ed.). (H. L. Ansbacher & R. R. Ansbacher, Eds.). New York: Viking Compass. (Original work published 1964)

Adler, A. (1980). *What life should mean to you*. (A. Porter, Ed.). New York: Perigee/G. P. Putnam. (Original work published 1931)

References

Adler, A. (2002). *The neurotic character*. (C. Koen, Trans.). H. T. Stein (Series Ed.). *Vol. 1*. San Francisco. (Original work published 1912)

Adler, K. A. (1963). *[Introduction]*. (See Adler, A., 1963.).

Ahlstrom, S. (1972). *A religious history of the American people*. New Haven: Yale University Press.

Ansbacher, H. L. (Ed.). (1966). Contributors to this issue. *American Journal of Individual Psychology, 22*(2), 152.

Ansbacher, H. L. (1985, Spring). In reference to Joseph Meiers and belonging. [Letter to the Editor]. *Individual Psychology Reporter, 3*(3), p. 7.

Ansbacher, H. L. (1990). Alfred Adler's influences on the three leading cofounders of Humanistic Psychology. *Journal of Humanistic Psychology, 30*(4), 45-53.

Ansbacher, H. L. (1992). Alfred Adler's concepts of community feeling and of social interest and the relevance of community feeling for old age. *Individual Psychology: The Journal of Adlerian Theory, Research and Practice, 48*(4), 402-412.

Bacon, F. (1620). *Novum organum: The new logic or true directions for the interpretation of nature* [Electronic version]. Retrieved April 6, 2007 from http://www.seop.leeds.ac.uk/entries/francis-bacon/#5

Beecher, M., & Beecher, W. (1972). *The mark of Cain: An anatomy of jealousy*. Richardson, TX: Beecher Foundation.

Belove, L. (1980). First encounters of the close kind (FECK): The use of the story of the first interaction as an early recollection of a marriage. *Journal of Individual Psychology, 36*(2), 191-208.

Bottome, P. (1939). *Alfred Adler: A biography*. New York: G. P. Putnam.

Carich, M. S. (1997). Variations of the 'as if' technique. In J. Carlson & S. Slavik (Eds.), *Techniques in Adlerian Psychology* (pp. 153-160). Washington, DC: Accelerated Development.

Carlson, J., Watts, R. E., & Maniacci, M. P. (2006). *Adlerian therapy: Theory and practice*. Washington, DC: American Psychological Association.

Cartwright, R. D. (1977). *Night life: Explorations in dreaming*. Upper Saddle River, NJ: Prentice-Hall.

Christensen, O. C. (Ed.). (2004). *Adlerian family counseling* (3rd ed.). Minneapolis, MN: Educational Media.

References

Clark, A. J. (2002). *Early recollections: Theory and practice in counseling and psychotherapy*. New York: Brunner-Routledge.

Clark, K. B. (1967). Implications of Adlerian theory for an understanding of civil rights problems and action. [Keynote Speech, 15th Annual Conference of the American Society of Adlerian Psychology, New York, NY]. *Journal of Individual Psychology, 23*(2), 181-190.

Dinkmeyer, D. C., Dinkmeyer, D. C., Jr., & Sperry, L. (1987). *Adlerian counseling and psychotherapy* (2nd ed.). Columbus, OH: Merrill.

Dinkmeyer, D. C., Jr., & McKay, G. D. (1998). *STEP/Teen.* Bowling Green, KY: STEP.

Dinkmeyer, D. C., Jr., & Sperry, L. (2000). *Counseling and psychotherapy: An integrated Individual Psychology approach* (3rd ed.). Columbus, OH: Merrill.

Dreikurs, R. (1949). *Fundamentals of Adlerian Psychology* (Rev. ed.). Chicago: Adler School of Professional Psychology. (Original work published 1933)

Dreikurs, R. (with Soltz, V.). (1964). *Children: The Challenge*. New York: Hawthorn.

Dreikurs, R. (1967). *Psychodynamics, psychotherapy, and counseling.* Chicago: Alfred Adler Institute.

Dreikurs, R., & Grey, L. (1968). *Logical consequences: A new approach to discipline*. New York: Meredith.

Dreikurs, R. (1971). *Social equality: The challenge of today.* Chicago: Henry Regnery.

Dreikurs, R. (1973). *Psychodynamics, psychotherapy and counseling: Collected papers of Rudolf Dreikurs, M. D.* (Rev.ed.). Chicago: Alfred Adler Institute.

Dreikurs, R. (1974). *Child guidance and education: Collected papers.* Chicago: Alfred Adler Institute.

Dreikurs, R., Gould, S., & Corsini, R. J. (1974). *Family council: The Dreikurs technique for putting an end to war between parents and children (and between children and children).* Chicago: Henry Regnery.

Dreikurs R., Shulman, B. H., & Mosak, H. H. (1984). *Mutiple psychotherapy: The use of two therapists with one patient.* Chicago: Alfred Adler Institute.

Eckstein, D., Baruth, L., & Mahrer, D. (1982). *Life style: What it is and how to do it.* Dubuque, IA: Kendall-Hall.

Edgerton, J. E., & Campbell, R. J. (Eds.). (1994). *American psychiatric glossary* (7th ed.). Washington, DC: American Psychiatric Press. [Electronic version]. Retrieved March 14, 2007, from http://www.webref.org/psychology/e/ego_boundaries.htm

References

Fausto-Sterling, A. (1993). The five sexes: Why male and female are not enough. *The Sciences, 33*(2), 20-25.

Ferguson, E. D. (2007). Work relations and work effectiveness: Goal identification and social interest can be learned. *Journal of Individual Psychology, 63*(1), 110-117.

Ganz, M. (1953). *The psychology of Alfred Adler and the development of the child.* London: Routledge & Kegan Paul. (Original work published 1935)

Gawande, A. (2007, April 30). The way we age now. *The New Yorker, LXXXIII(10),* 50-59.

Goodman, P. (1969). *The politics of being queer.* [Essay]. [Electronic version]. Retrieved January 15, 2007, from http//en.wikipedia.org/wiki./Paul_Goodman_%28writer%29

Griffith, J. (1984). Adler's organ jargon. *Individual Psychology, 40*(4), 437-444.

Grunwald, B. B., & McAbee, H. V. (1999). *Guiding the family: Practical counseling solutions* (2nd ed.). Philadelphia: Accelerated Development.

Harre, R., & Lamb, R. (Eds.). (1983). *Encyclopedic dictionary of psychology.* Cambridge, MA: MIT Press.

Hoffman, E. (1994). *The drive for self: Alfred Adler and the founding of Individual Psychology.* Reading, MA: Addison-Wesley.

Horney, K. (1945). *Our inner conflicts: A constructive theory of neurosis.* New York: Norton.

Hunt, M. (1993). *The story of psychology.* New York: Bantam.

Ingersoll, R. G. (1833-1899). [Quotation]. Retrieved March 4, 2007 from http://www.quotationspage.com/quotes/Robert_Ingersoll/

Kefir, N., & Corsini, R. J. (1974). Dispositional sets: A contribution to typology. *Journal of Individual Psychology, 30*(2), 163-178.

Kern, R. M., Hawes, E. C., & Christianson, O. C. (1989). *Couples therapy: An Adlerian perspective.* Minneapolis, MN: Educational Media.

Lazarsfeld, S. (1966). The courage for imperfection. *American Journal of Individual Psychology, 22*(2), 163-165.

Manaster, G. J., & Corsini, R. J. (1982). *Individual Psychology: Theory and practice.* Itasca, IL: F. E. Peacock.

Maniacci, M., Shulman, B., Griffith, J., Powers, R. L., Sutherland, J., Dushman, R., & Schneider, M. F. (1998). Early recollections: Mining the personal story in the process of change. *Journal of Individual Psychology, 54*(4), 451-479.

References

McKay, G. D., & Maybell, S. A. (2004). *Calming the family storm: Anger management for moms, dads, and all the kids.* Atascadero, CA: Impact

Merriam Webster's collegiate dictionary (10th ed.). (1993). Springfield, MA: Merriam-Webster.

Mosak, H. H. (1977). *On purpose: Collected papers.* Chicago: Adler School of Professional Psychology.

Modzierz, G. J., Macchitelli, F. J., & Lisieki, J. (1976). The paradox in psychotherapy: An Adlerian perspective. *Journal of Individual Psychology, 32*(2), 169-184.

Nelsen, J. (1996). *Positive discipline.* New York: Ballantine.

Oberst, U. E., & Stewart, A. E. (2003). *Adlerian psychotherapy: An advanced approach to Individual Psychology.* New York: Brunner-Routledge.

Orgler, H. (1963). *Alfred Adler: The man and his work.* New York: Liveright.

Painter, G., & Corsini, R. J. (1990). *Effective discipline in home and school.* Muncie, IN: Accelerated Development.

Platt, J. M. (1989). *Life in the family zoo.* Sacramento, CA: Dynamic Training and Seminars.

Popkin, M. H. (1993). *Active parenting today.* Kennesaw, GA: Active Parenting.

Powers, R. L. (1973). Myth and memory. In H. H. Mosak (Ed.), *Alfred Adler: His influence on psychology today* (pp. 271-290). Park Ridge, NJ: Noyes.

Powers, R. L. (2003). Robert L. Powers's original contribution to "Spirituality in the Adlerian forum." *Journal of Individual Psychology*, *59*(1), pp. 83-85.

Powers, R. L., & Griffith, J. (1982). Psycho-clarity: Another view of the goal of therapy. *Individual Psychology Reporter, 1*(1), 1.

Powers, R. L., & Griffith, J. (1986). The "big numbers": Gender guiding lines and expectations. *Individual Psychology Reporter, 4*(2), 1, 6.

Powers, R. L., & Griffith, J. (1987). *Understanding life-style: The psycho-clarity process.* Port Townsend, WA: Adlerian Psychology Associates.

Powers, R. L., & Griffith, J. (1992). More on the "big numbers." *Individual Psychology Reporter, 9*(4), 1-2.

Powers, R. L., & Griffith, J. (1995). *The Individual Psychology client workbook with supplements.* Port Townsend, WA: Adlerian Psychology Associates.

References

Powers, R. L., & Griffith, J. (1996). Enhancing the quality of Adlerian life: An assessment and reorientation. [Keynote Speech, 42nd Annual Conference of the North American Society of Adlerian Psychology, San Diego CA]. *Individual Psychology, 52*(1), 3-21.

Powers, R. L., Griffith, J., & Maybell, S.A. (1993). Gender guiding lines and couples therapy. *Individual Psychology, 49*(3 & 4), 361-371.

Robb, M. (1932). Organ jargon. *Individual Psychology Medical Pamphlets, 4,* 61-67.

Selye, H. (1978). *The stress of life* (Rev. ed.). New York: McGraw-Hill. (Original work published 1956)

Sherman, R., & Fredman, N. (1986). *Handbook of structured techniques in marriage and family therapy.* New York: Brunner/Mazel.

Shulman, B. H. (1973). *Contributions to Individual Psychology: Selected papers.* Chicago: Alfred Adler Institute.

Shulman, B. H., & Mosak, H. H. (1988). *Manual for life style assessment.* Chicago: Alfred Adler Institute.

Sicher, L. (1955). Education for freedom. *American Journal of Individual Psychology, 11,* 92- 203.

Sicher, L. (1991). *The collected works of Lydia Sicher: An Adlerian perspective.* (A. K. Davidson, Ed.). Ft. Bragg, CA: QED Press.

Smuts, J. (1961). *Holism and evolution.* New York: Viking. (Original work published 1926)

Sonstegard, M. A., & Bitter, J. R. (with Pelonis, P.). (2004). *Adlerian group counseling and therapy: Step-by-step.* New York: Brunner-Routledge.

Sperry, L., & Carlson, J. (1993). *Psychopathology and psychotherapy from diagnosis to treatment.* Muncie: IN: Accelerated Development.

Stein, H. (2002). (Series Ed.). *The collected clinical works of Alfred Adler, Vol. 1.* (C. Koen, Trans.) San Francisco: Alfred Adler Institute of San Francisco. (Original work published 1912)

Sweeney, T. J. (1989). *Adlerian counseling: A practical approach for a new decade (3rd ed.).* Muncie, IN: Accelerated Development.

Terner, J., & Pew, W. L. (1978). *The courage to be imperfect: The life and work of Rudolf Dreikurs.* New York: Hawthorn.

Vaihinger, H. (1968). *The philosophy of "as if": A system of the theoretical, practical and religious fictions of mankind.* (C. K. Ogden, Trans.). New York: Barnes and Noble. (Original work published 1911)

References

Walton, F. X., & Powers, R. L. (1974). *Winning children over*. Columbia, SC: Adlerian Child Care Books.

Walton, F. X. (1980). *Winning teenagers over at home and school*. Columbia, SC: Adlerian Child Care Books.

Walton, F. X. (1990). Use of the most memorable observation as a technique for understanding choice of parenting style. *Journal of Individual Psychology*, *54*(4), 487-494.

Walton, F. X. (producer & director) (1996). The use of the most memorable observation in counseling and parent consultation [video].

Wexberg, E. (1970). *Individual Psychological treatment*. (A. Eiloart, Trans.). (Revised and annotated by B. H. Shulman.). Chicago: Alfred Adler Institute. (Original work published 1929)

INDEX

A (general index cont'd from page 118)

myths of the peoples, 26

N

NATURAL, LOGICAL CONSEQUENCES, 71
nature, nurture, 51
Nazi pseudo-philosophy, 106
Nazis, 54
"needs," 90
negationary tactics (PARADOX), 78
negative bias, 8
"neither heredity nor environment," 97
Nelsen, J., 79
neologism, 35, 83
nervous tic, 78
neurosis and psychosis, 68
NEUROSIS: "YES, BUT . . .", 72
neurotic arrangements, 7
The Neurotic Character, 54
neurotic movement, 4, 5, 8, 11, 13, 14, 19, 20,
    22, 48, 50, 52, 67, 68, 72, 89, 91, 105, 106
Nietzsche, F., 106
NORMAL, ABNORMAL, 73
    community feeling as standard, 73
normality, 14
normative assessment, 17
norms 10, 43
"NOT ME!" (SOCIOPATHY), 96

O

Oberst, U. E., 11, 84
occupation, life task, 11
    adolescent challenge, 12
Omnia ad opinionem suspensa sunt (L.), 80
only child, 24
OPEN FORUM FAMILY COUNSELING, 74
opinion, "Everything depends upon opinion"
    (Seneca),", 80
ORGAN DIALECT, ORGAN JARGON, ORGAN
    LANGUAGE, 40, 75
ORGAN INFERIORITY, 12, 76
    childhood disorders, 1
Orgler, H., 73
orientation, 15
OVERBURDENING CHILDHOOD SITUATIONS, 1,
    65, 76, 77
overcoming, aggression drive, 3
OVER-COMPENSATION, see COMPENSATION
oversensitivity, 89

P

Painter, G., 27
Papal infallibility doctrine (1870), 54
pampered child, 18
pampered styles of life, 22
panic attacks, 89
PARADOX, 78
    Adler as innovator, 78
paralysis, 89
PARENTING, 2, 10, 22, 27, 36, 69A, 79, 94

pattern
    factophilia, 35
    of a child's life, 29
    of movement, 37
    of neurotic functioning, 13, 90
peer acceptance, 2
Pelonis, P., 47
penis envy, see Freud
Pepper, F., 27
perception, field of, 6, 10
perfection, 3
    concretized in God, 45
    goal of evolution, 32
    striving for, 32
Perls, F., 5, 90
persona (L.), character mask, 92
personal development, 10, 17, 28, 58, 84, 103
personality, 1, 7, 34, 37
    priorities, 103
    self-consistent, 58
personality ideal, see SELF-IDEAL
PERSÖNLICHKEITSIDEAL (G.), see SELF-IDEAL
perversion ("wrong turn"), 93
Pew, W. L., 19, 47, 74, 102
phainomenon (Gr.), 80
phases of psychotherapy, 1
PHENOMENOLOGY, 6, 12, 22, 80
philosophy, 8, 33
The Philosophy of 'As If', 8
place, in family, 84
    in group, 56
Platt, J. M., 79
Plessy v. Ferguson, 30
plus, from minus to, 69
Popkin, M. H., 79
POSSESSION, PSYCHOLOGY OF, 85
power, 11, 24, 71, 93, 106
power struggle, 71
Powers, R. L, 10, 26, 31, 36, 37, 43, 45, 47,
    51, 55, 62, 69, 79, 97, 103
    neologism, 83
    psychoclarity, 81
*The Practice and Theory of Individual
    Psychology*, 7
prejudice, 6, 12
pretend ("AS IF"), 8
PRIORITIES, see TYPES
PRIVATE LOGIC, 48, 49, 67, 81, 83, 90
PRIVATE MEANING, see PRIVATE LOGIC
PRIVATE SENSE VS. COMMON SENSE, 81, see
    PRIVATE LOGIC
problems of life, 64, 85, see LIFE TASKS
problem-solving, 4, 38
PROFESSIONAL RESPONSIBILITY, 82
    doctor's, 4
    patient's, 1
psychiatry, 83
psychic activities, goal of, 44
"psychical superstructure," 12
Psychoanalysis, 2, 3, 4

About the Authors

Jane Griffith, MA, MAT, is a professor *emerita* of the Adler School of Professional Psychology, Chicago, and a licensed clinical professional counselor. Robert L. Powers, MDiv, MA, is the distinguished service professor in Adlerian Studies in Culture and Personality, *emeritus*, of the School, and a licensed clinical psychologist. Each is a past-president and *Diplomate* of the North American Society of Adlerian Psychology. In addition to the present volume, *The Lexicon of Adlerian Psychology,* they are coauthors of *Understanding Life-Style: The Psycho-Clarity Process*, a text in Adlerian personality assessment, and its accompanying *Individual Psychology Client Workbook*, as well as numerous professional articles. They serve as column editors for Biopsychosocial Issues for the *Journal of Individual Psychology.* They have lectured and taught in North America and abroad, and currently teach a four-course certificate program in Adlerian Psychology for the Puget Sound Adlerian Society. They are married to each other and live in Port Townsend, Washington.

CPSIA information can be obtained
at www.ICGtesting.com
Printed in the USA
BVHW06s0041090718
521075BV00002B/5/P